EVONNE!

EVONNE!
On the Move

Evonne Goolagong with Bud Collins

E. P. DUTTON & CO., INC. | NEW YORK | 1975

Published simultaneously in Canada
by Clarke, Irwin & Company Limited, Toronto and Vancouver

Library of Congress Cataloging in Publication Data

Goolagong, Evonne, 1951–
Evonne! On the move.
1. Goolagong, Evonne, 1951–   2. Tennis.
I. Collins, Bud, joint author. II. Title.
GV994.G67A34   796.34′2′0924   74-3245
ISBN: 0-525-10115-2

For the three men in my life

My Dad—Kenneth Goolagong
My Coach and Dad No. 2—Vic Edwards
and
My original mentor—Bill Kurtzman

Prologue

Here she was, trembling. And here we were, curious and expectant. We'd read about her, heard about her, and now . . . now . . . Ladies and Gentlemen—the Great Dark Hope—Evonne Goolagong! Of course it wasn't like that at Wimbledon on that overcast afternoon late in June of 1970.

Nobody is announced at Wimbledon. They just appear, and the patrons know who they are. They were twenty-one-year-old Jane (Peaches) Bartkowicz of Hamtramck, Michigan, ranked No. 6 in her country, and eighteen-year-old Evonne Goolagong of Sydney, Australia, ranked No. 6 in hers, put onto Centre Court for a second-round match. Neither one of them had a hope of going much further in this ultimate tennis tournament, and so neither was disappointed— Evonne by defeat that day or Peaches by defeat the next.

The reason they were out there on the show court was quite simple: everybody wanted a look at the girl from the bush whose manner and moves were beginning to captivate the tennis public. A year later Evonne would return to knock the place dead and win it all, but now she was so scared walking onto Centre that she wondered if she could walk at all. Then it was a forbidding place lined with 14,000 faces—but it would become her turf, populated with her people, terribly anxious for her to win.

Evonne was on her first trip away from Australia, new to the world, the beneficiary of a grapevine build-up from other players and Australian reporters: "Wait'll you see this Goolagong kid." I'd waited, ready to become a believer—which I did—but not a believer in invincibility or a new Strongarm Annie in the style of Margaret Court or Billie Jean King or Chrissie Evert. The belief is in an experience—of beholding grace and athleticism and joy in a performance, and of going away feeling better for it.

As Evonne fidgeted and fumbled through that sixteen-game loss to Bartkowicz, the Beatles tune "Something" ("something in the way she moves") went through my mind, and—it didn't take a genius to perceive it—like everybody else in the stadium I knew I was watching a rare young woman with the soul of a true athlete. It is customary to say, "She's the next . . ." or "She's another . . . ," and the comparison usually was with the majestic Maria Bueno, who had won Wimbledon three times between 1959 and 1964. Complimentary but inaccurate: Evonne isn't the next or another anybody—she's the Singular Goolagong. For all her speed, power, and feline maneuvering, it's her nature that sets her apart. Human is human, and Evonne isn't any more or less human than any of her colleagues. Yet her naturalness in beaming that humanity—the smile, the good-natured shrug, the tiny shriek when she's made a mistake, her obvious feeling that it's really only a game—wins love from an audience that deals out only admiration to the others. She works Wimbledon and the other big gigs as though she were a kid playing in a meadow. She doesn't know why or how—she just does. And, too, as tennis has become a world of such high finance and pressure, perhaps this carefree mood of hers seems even more precious to us.

After her first Wimbledon defeat by Bartkowicz, Evonne met with the reporters. She was not the lighthearted sunshine girl. She was shy and withdrawn. There were a lot of us for one thing, and she wasn't good on her feet when confronted by so many new and inquisitive faces. We wanted to talk about race. She didn't. Could she understand what Arthur Ashe had been through? She'd never met Arthur Ashe. Would she tell us about this extraordinary background of hers, about growing up in the Outback? To her it wasn't so extraordinary

8

—and she wasn't from the Outback. She was from the country. The interview dragged; and finally and mercifully her manager–coach–discoverer-substitute-father Vic Edwards ended it, sent her off, and sat down with reporters to supply more facts. "She'll be all right with you boys one of these days," Vic said, and he was right, as he has been about most things concerned with his find. Vic and his wife Eva have been very protective of Evonne, bringing her along slowly. Now she handles interviews like any seasoned pro, but she gets edgy if they go on for very long. She doesn't feel there's that much to say about anything, or that she's that big a deal. Frankly, she has questioned whether this book, about a woman so young, should even be written.

Julie Heldman, a competitor of Evonne's and a sharp observer, cautioned American reporters, "Don't expect the kind of eighteen year old you talk to at home. Evonne is very unsophisticated, she's three, maybe five years behind an eighteen-year-old American in the ways of the world, which is part of her charm." Evonne has grown up a lot, but the uncomplicated girlishness remains.

A few days before Evonne was born in 1951, an American named Doris Hart won Wimbledon. Undoubtedly, the latter event went totally unnoticed by Melinda and Ken Goolagong in the dry, dusty, dreary sheep country several hundred miles from Sydney—and several light years from anything in their experience and imagination. Neither Melinda nor Ken had ever seen a tennis ball before Ken came across a few of them in the back seat of a used jalopy he bought when Evonne was a baby.

It would be a good story—true, even—to report infant Evonne's immediate fascination with those scuffed balls. Prophetic, maybe? An omen, like the boy Mozart fingering the piano keys? Not quite. The Mozarts knew their way around music. The Goolagongs, way out in their one-saloon town of Barellan, in the vastness of New South Wales, were blissfully unaware of the game of tennis. Although Evonne has become a champion, her parents have never taken much interest in tennis. It's a diversion foreign to their existence as Aborigines, descendants of the original Australians, who—like the American Indians—were pushed under the rug, shoved to the wrong side of society's tracks, and at times willfully slaughtered. Aborigines haven't had much of a shot in the country that originally belonged to them. The odds against any of them making it in tennis—a very white game, with a few exceptions—are so great that only one has succeeded: Evonne.

All you have to know about Australians is that they love sport nearly as much as beer. An Australian would go crazy having to choose between them. Australians are born with bent elbows, which may explain how they put so much spin on their serves. However, Aborigines, living on the fringe, hardly ever encouraged to compete, haven't made much impact in the sporting scene. Only in recent years have they been tolerated at the national pastime and been permitted in the pubs for a grog-up.

As a dominant force in tennis playing as well as beer drinking, Australians grew used to their own conquering Wimbledon and standing as world champions. A line of male champs began with Norman Brookes prior to World War I and continued following World War II with Frank Sedgman, Lew Hoad, Ken Rosewall, Ashley Cooper, Neale Fraser, Rod Laver, Roy Emerson, and John Newcombe. Then there was Margaret Smith Court, winner of more major titles than anybody ever. Australians became the Tennis Mafia.

But Evonne was different, singular. She gave the line another hue. She was the authentic Australian, with the skin and the name that made the rest of them seem foreigners. Years before, some of her people had probably met Captain Cook on the shore and thought him a milk-white-looking alien.

Twenty years after the arrivals of Goolagong and Hart—Evonne on earth, Doris on hallowed sod as a Wimbledon winner—Mr. and Mrs. Goolagong were excitedly realizing what their child was about. Maybe they weren't tennis buffs or Wimbledon devotees, but in 1971 they sat nervously, in the company of millions of others across the world in front of television sets, observing their surprising offspring, as Evonne lifted the championship from Margaret Court. Melinda and Ken knew enough by this time to be impressed that by passing the supreme test in the game (two weeks of Wimbledon) their kid was on top of the world. Melinda, hypertensive anyway, felt her blood pressure going higher. Ken, normally reticent, had two or three beers and was the life of the television party that night in their small, linoleum-floored living room in Barellan. Had parents ever been less suspecting of what would become of their child?

For those who watched Hart win Wimbledon in 1951 and Goolagong win it a generation later, either by viewing it on television or stuffed into the imposing Centre Court arena, the panorama appeared unchanged. The place, as always, was sold out well in advance, and three thousand customers had lined up outside the grounds the night before for the pleasure of occupying standing room. The standees and the 11,000 seated patrons surrounded a grass court fastidiously coiffed by Bob Twynam (groundsman for a half-century), a patch of green that superior tennis players have sought to master since 1921, when the "new" Wimbledon opened to continue the world's oldest tournament. The hemlines of Goolagong and Court were higher than those of Hart and her finalist, Shirley Fry, and you wouldn't have seen any jeans and sandals in the crowd of 1951. But Evonne lifted the golden platter, the symbol of rule, as high as Doris had during her equally prideful coronation two decades before. Hart says, "That's the moment you've worked for and thought about for all those hours, all those years."

The tableau at Wimbledon was the same. Behind it, though, everything in 1971 was as different as Evonne. Hart was an amateur. Goolagong was a professional. The distinction is subtle because there were no professional women as such in 1951, and none of the major tournaments offered prize money, whereas in 1971 few of the ninety-six women entered at Wimbledon were nonprofessionals, and Evonne's first prize was $4,320. In actuality, Hart was a professional amateur, as were most of her colleagues, male and female, at that time. Tennis was as much her life as it is Evonne's; she worked as hard at it. Forthright pros—the sprinkling of men such as Pancho Gonzalez and Jack Kramer—were not welcome at Wimbledon. Not until 1968 did the hypocrisy in the form of expense money as payment to amateurs cease with the acceptance of open tennis and monetary prizes based on winning.

11

There was more to the transition from amateurism to professionalism than money and status. Suddenly mores that had been unchanged for almost a century were disrupted. Players were no longer the chattel of a private club establishment that ran the national tennis associations, nor were they expected to perform as little ladies and gentleman lest they lose their travel privileges and no longer be welcome at the restricted clubs where the most distinguished events took place. Even after she had won at Forest Hills and Wimbledon, Afro-American Althea Gibson was not welcome to play at numerous clubs in her own country.

In America reputations were made in a tight circle of summer grass tournaments held at patrician clubs along the Eastern Seaboard —places such as the Maidstone Club at East Hampton, New York; the Essex County Club at Manchester, Massachusetts; the Merion Cricket Club at Haverford, Pennsylvania; the Orange Lawn Tennis Club at South Orange, New Jersey. Except for the National's at Forest Hills, tennis wasn't really a public game. The tournaments at these secluded hideaways were staged for the benefit of members and guests. Tennis Week was the highlight of a club's summer season, and the players were expected to show their gratitude for being housed and fed by acting as window dressing at the nightly parties, sometimes playing tennis with their hosts, or baby-sitting. The most influential club members had their pick of the "name" players as houseguests, and they showed them off like baubles on a charm bracelet.

Rankings were based on results in the East, travel and "expenses" were based on rankings, and appearance and decorum, rather than ability, were too often the basis for rankings. Billie Jean King recalls, "Even though I was the best junior in my section (Southern California) the trips east often went to others who were better liked by the officials. The officials were always men."

A week at a place like Essex County Club, on the sea north of Boston in bucolic Brahmin country, could be a marvelous respite: sailing, horseback riding, clambakes, shopping in exclusive stores, plenty of college boys to date. The name of the tournament itself— the last singles tune-up prior to Forest Hills—had the ring of another era: the Ladies' Invitational. Nice, comfortable if you were on summer vacation from school, but hardly a way to build a career. But, then, the players weren't supposed to. Those who kept coming back year after year—the professional amateurs who hadn't married and settled down—weren't treated kindly by tennis gossipers. For one thing, the older women weren't as starry-eyed and manageable as the incoming teen-agers. Still, unless they had independent incomes, they, too, had to play the rankings game and be politic to officials and club members who counted. A lot of players came out of country clubs themselves and moved comfortably on the circuit. Darlene Hard, a champion of the late 1950s from a working-class background, said, "Because these people allow you in their clubs and tournaments, they sometimes act like they own you." In a way they did. "They think your time is theirs, and that you're around for their entertainment."

That era and its atmosphere were destroyed by open tennis. Now rankings mean little. "The only thing that counts is the prize money you win," says Valerie Ziegenfuss. "We should be ranked on dollars like in golf." The Eastern grass circuit is dead. Those clubs were neither inclined nor equipped to handle large prize-money events, and, with the exception of Forest Hills and one or two other lucrative tourneys, the tennis centers today are indoor arenas, catering to crowds larger, broader, and more enthusiastic than those elite hundreds at the retreats of the rich.

Tennis, suffering from a reputation as a rich person's game, came out of the country club closet and went public. Not only for the pros, but for The Public. An A.C. Nielsen survey of late 1974 set the number of tennis-playing Americans at an incredible 34 million!

In 1968 a new future abruptly opened for a female athlete who could hit a tennis ball; she could have a respected career with the opportunity to earn well and be widely recognized. The ascendancy of women in sports is nowhere as dramatic as in tennis. Billie Jean King was the first female athlete to hit the $100,000 mark in prize money in 1971, and Margaret Court the first at $200,000 in 1973. Chrissie Evert topped both by winning $238,585 in 1974 (when Goolagong did $101,000).

Now a woman could develop her athleticism and talent, persevere in a field she loved, and, if she continued after, say, age twenty-two, not be described as a "tennis bum." That was a common appellation used in the phony amateur days for adult men who didn't get a "real job" or for women who failed to retire to domesticity. The stigma was gone, and the women, at last, were in business.

For feminist Billie Jean King, it was "a chance to fulfill myself without having to follow the stereotype of quitting to have a home and babies."

For nonfeminist Margaret Court, who (unlike King) maintained a close at-home-on-the-road relationship with her baby-sitting husband, Barry, and performed even more convincingly after the birth of her first child, it was "seeing how good I could get by being able to play in the prime years, the late twenties and early thirties."

For Wendy Overton, a young American on the pro tour, it was "a way of life I didn't expect to be able to follow. When I went to college, it was, you know, socially approved to play the summer tournaments and see the world on tennis. But when I got out in '69 most of my friends were getting married. If you didn't, you got a job. Open tennis was here, but there wasn't that much money in it except for the stars—Billie Jean, Rosie Casals, Margaret, Ann Jones, and a few others. I was working as a secretary, and the money in tennis was getting better. In '71 I decided to try it on the Virginia Slims tour. My folks thought I was a little foolish. There was no guarantee I'd make a dime. But I won a little that year, and $30,000 the next, and that was it—I'm a pro."

Billie Jean says, "This is very recent. It didn't exist when I was coming up, or even when Evonne began to travel [King is eight years older than Goolagong]. Can you imagine what this is doing to kids nine and ten years old now, knowing they can become professionals? What crops are coming up! This game is just beginning for women. Professional is an honored word in America; it's what I always wanted to be. But tennis was run by a lot of stuffy people who were way behind the times. If a baseball player was respected as a pro, why shouldn't I be as a tennis pro? That's what frustrated me. But tennis didn't operate that way—then. You were supposed to be happy as a so-called amateur, playing for small crowds at private clubs, accepting whatever expense money was left over for the women. To be truthful, in my last amateur days I was getting plenty, as much as $1,200 a week —because I was the best—but the pretense got me.

"The American public isn't interested in amateurs. That's small-time. Tennis was small-time, but I knew it could be big-time if we'd open it up, go into larger arenas, bring in prize money. Then everybody would have a chance at money a lot bigger than I was taking under the table as an amateur."

Ever straightforward, and too vocal for the officials who controlled the amateur game (as tennis was organized in the pre-1968 era), Billie Jean was always in trouble and frequently suspended. She was a refreshing zephyr of honesty in 1967 when she kept insisting, "Don't call me an amateur. That's a dirty word, a technicality. I'm a pro no matter what the rules say. This is my life, tennis, and I want to be thought of as a pro. Let's have prize money, not 'expenses' and 'appearance fees.' " Her attitude helped bring down a bogus system that was crying for reform.

Of course, King's evangelism on behalf of the women, and tennis as a whole, was a prime factor in the growth of the game as a vocational opportunity for the doers and a significant entertainment for the watchers. She says, "When I won Wimbledon in 1966 and 1967 as an amateur only the people concerned with tennis knew, and there weren't too many of them. When I won in 1972 and 1973 everybody interested in sports knew, and a lot more besides. You play for money, and the public takes you seriously." Her appearance in 1973 against the geriatric set's sex symbol, Bobby Riggs, didn't hurt either.

His Piggishness, Riggs, a Wimbledon champion of 1939 who had aged ungracefully to fifty-six, was out to have some fun at female expense and his own psychic enrichment when he began challenging the leading women pros to cohabit a tennis court for the purpose of intersexual singles. Margaret Court took the bait. Waddling yet cagey, Bobby took her with ease, psyching her out in a show biz setting for the glorification of a housing development at Ramona, California.

It was a haphazard but astonishingly successful promotion by the developers and a Hollywood agent, but there would be nothing haphazard about the follow-up: Billie Jean versus Bobby at the Astrodome in Houston. It was hyped to the skies like a heavyweight title fight involving Muhammad Ali and became an international happening, the ultimate in male-female combat since Perseus had it out with Medusa—or so a lot of otherwise rational people seemed to think. It was gawdy, tasteless, and cuckoo, but it was also entertaining, and it drew the largest tennis crowd ever, 30,472 plus the millions hanging out at television sets. There was no title at stake. It really meant nothing competitively—a verbose, washed-up geezer against a verbose, active pro—but it meant plenty financially: several hundred thousand dollars in endorsements for both of them and $100,000 added for the victor. Nevertheless, for the first time everybody was interested in a game of tennis. That occasion did more to stimulate attention for an already rising sport than anything before. And the fact that a superbly trained Billie Jean murdered His Piggishness, who was stuffed with hubris and hype, added immeasurable luster to the women's professional game.

"You've come a long way baby," the advertising slogan of Virginia Slims cigarettes, was shrewdly carried to the public by the female pros after Joe Cullman, a tennis nut who presides over the parent company, Philip Morris, decided his firm would underwrite the first full-fledged women's tour in 1971. Until then women were merely afterthoughts in the newly created universe of open tennis, taking the short end of the prize money as they had "expenses" in the amateur age. In 1968, as tennis officials cautiously tested the atmosphere of opens, twelve such events were sanctioned throughout the world (today there are hundreds). The biggest financially was the $100,000 U.S. Open at Forest Hills, at which 80 percent of the prize money was allotted to men. First prize for men was $14,000; Virginia Wade collected $6,000 as champion woman. The disparity was even greater in other tournaments, and Ann Jones, then No. 1 in Britain, declined to enter the very first open in history, the British Hard

Courts at Bournemouth, because first prize for women was $720 compared to $2,400 for men.

By the end of 1970 the women were griping openly and bitterly about their unfair treatment at the pay window. A number of them, led by Billie Jean, held a press conference at Forest Hills to discuss a possible boycott of the Pacific Southwest Open at Los Angeles, where prize money ratio was to be about 12 to 1. Gail Chanfreau, the No. 1 French player, whose husband played Davis Cup for France, wondered, "Why aren't we getting consideration in distribution of prize money? I work as hard at this game as my husband. I train as hard, try as hard, I'm under the same tournament pressures. I realize we won't get equal prize money, but the way things are going it is very unfair."

The male attitude was chauvinistically expressed by Arthur Ashe (who has since recanted somewhat): "They should realize we men are earning livings, supporting families. We're the drawing cards and should get most of the money. They don't draw flies."

But Esmé Emanuel and Cecilia Martinez, two players out of San Francisco State University, said they'd conducted a survey among a crowd of 13,000 in the Forest Hills Stadium, and they offered this finding: "Fifty-four percent of the men we polled said they thought women's tennis was as interesting to watch as men's."

When the women did boycott the Southwest Open, which followed Forest Hills, their cause was taken up by Gladys Heldman, publisher of *World Tennis* magazine. Heldman enlisted the aid of Joe Cullman and sponsorship of Virginia Slims, forming the Slims circuit for 1971. This was the Big Breakaway. Neglected and knocked by the controllers of tennis—all male—the women decided to go it alone for nineteen tournaments in the United States. Whereas total prize money available to them all over the world in 1970 hadn't amounted to much more than $150,000, they were playing for nearly $200,000 on the Slims circuit in 1971. As the Slims purses ascended steadily to almost $1 million in 1974, that impetus drove up compensation everywhere so that an extraordinary pot of about $2 million overall was up there for

17

the women to strive for. Equality was out there in some places, too, notably Forest Hills, where 1974 champs Billie Jean King and Jimmy Connors received $22,500 and a new car apiece, and the money was the same for men and women right down the line. Sponsors other than Virginia Slims seemed to line up to give away money. *Family Circle* magazine put up $110,000 for a tournament at Sea Pines, South Carolina, and Chrissie Evert came away with $30,000 first prize. Chesebrough-Pond's beauty and health care division dangled $125,000 for any woman player who could win a Grand Slam (the opens of Australia, France, Britain [Wimbledon], and the U.S.). Nobody did, but Evert pocketed a $35,000 bonus for the best record in those events for 1974, with Evonne—winner of the Australian and runner-up in the U.S.—just behind.

Separation of the sexes for most tournaments had proved a bonanza for the women in several ways. Obviously they were earning handsomely, but they were also being recognized as sporting personalities in their own right, getting as much—and sometimes more —publicity than the men. In some locales they were outdrawing the men, and in others they were presenting major tennis for the first time. As tennis soared to fourth place from no place in public sporting interest (according to a Harris Poll of September 1974), the women soared right up there with the men. Readers of *Esquire* magazine, balloting for America's most popular jocks, named Joe Namath of football, Muhammad Ali of boxing, and Billie Jean!

In some respects the women were probably fortunate in being the weaker sex. They couldn't overpower tennis the way men did, and their matches didn't degenerate into serve-and-volley tedium. Their styles seemed more distinctive: the tiny whirling-dervish militant, Rosie Casals . . . the King Kong in skirts, Margaret Court . . . the Little Machine, Chrissie Evert . . . the serve-and-volleying Old Lady, Billie Jean King . . . the daydreaming natural, Evonne Goolagong . . . the psychedelic strokeswoman, Françoise Durr . . . the hip intellectual, Julie Heldman . . . the leader of the no-bra rebellion, Kristien Kemmer . . . the Kid Sister, Jeannie Evert . . . the tough Texan with blazing stare and forehand, Nancy Gunter . . . the queenly

Limie, Virginia Wade . . . the Volga Volleyer, Olga Morozova . . . the golden giraffe, Helga Masthoff . . .

Could a tennis nut identify with a Rod Laver, slamming the ball with such mesmerizing speed and precision? Maybe not, but you could feel rapport with Françoise Durr, laboring behind that popcorn-ball serve, and those hideous—yet deadly—homemade strokes that make her appear to be ladling soup amid a swarm of bees. There is a sameness to the thunder of the men's game where the foremost tactic is get to the net. Frequently the women are more entertaining. Strategy plays a greater role in their game. Their limitations become their strengths for many spectators who delight in watching patterns develop and enjoy the fact that female matches are less formful and shorter. Service breaks are frequent, comebacks from hopeless depths more likely.

The men are still grumbling about the U.S. Open submitting to demands for equal prize in 1974 from the recently organized female players union, the Women's Tennis Association. A common male argument: "They don't work as long or hard. We play best of five sets, they play best of three. We're the drawing cards." But do the customers pay for quality or quantity? Forest Hills 1974 was a solid argument for the women. On the second Thursday of play, a magnificent day, the men had the place practically to themselves and drew 14,916 for quarter-finals. The next day, cool and rainy, 13,017 appeared for the women's semifinals: Goolagong versus Evert; King versus Heldman. Furthermore, the final—King over Goolagong in a 3–6, 6–3, 7–5 gala —was considerably more gripping than Jimmy Connors's 6–1, 6–0, 6–1 slaughter of Ken Rosewall. Hackers in the audience could really connect as Evonne and Billie Jean darted corner to corner, up to the net, and deep behind the baseline to keep the ball going back and forth during incredible rallies. One point Evonne won late in the third set on a fantastic series of retrieves and lobs was the most electrifying I have witnessed, transporting the full-house mob of 15,300 into one unending shriek as the scrambling and shotmaking went beyond the believable.

As many memorable women's matches as men's skitter about in

my brain, but none more excruciating than Evonne's revival from a set down and 0–3 in the second to beat Chrissie Evert in that Wimbledon semifinal of 1972, the inaugural of their Rivalry of the Seventies.

The money will go up along with the standard. As Billie Jean points out, there's a vast menagerie of wonderplayers enroute to the big league.

In Doris Hart's day, the only option for a player who wished to make a steady living in tennis was teaching. Hart became a teaching pro and still is. Her doubles partner, Shirley Fry Irvin, who won the Wimbledon singles in 1956, says, "There was a very small, token money prize at Wimbledon then. So small I can't remember what it was. Maybe £10. They gave you expenses, and the U.S. Lawn Tennis Association bought you a plane ticket to London—but only if you were one of the very top women. There wasn't the opportunity then, no outlet for playing professionally." Shirley, a Hartford housewife with four children who moonlights as a tennis instructor, continues: "We made a living on the circuit then, Doris Hart and I. I mean, at the top the expenses were sufficient to feed and clothe us and keep us traveling for a short time. But I didn't make any money over. I had to work at other jobs when we weren't playing. We didn't play as many tournaments, fourteen or so, and most of the important ones were on grass at small prestigious clubs in the Northeast. It was mainly a summer game, with a few winter tournaments in the Caribbean. There wasn't any indoor circuit.

"Now they can play fifty-two weeks of the year if they can hold up. Sure I would like to have done it. With my kids to send to college, I would have liked to put some money away. But," she says, "I wonder if they have as much fun as we did? There's more physical and mental pressure now with all the tournaments and all the money. It's more competitive, no doubt of that. I don't think they rest enough, but it's understandable. If you don't play, you don't earn.

"We just looked at it differently. It was a temporary life," says Shirley, who, at twenty-nine, stopped playing major tennis later than most of her contemporaries. "But it couldn't be a career." Not unless you were wealthy, like Margaret duPont. Shirley feels, "Maybe we

20

appreciated what we got more then because not so much was available to us. Look at it now—not only the big-money tournaments but World Team Tennis. Maybe," she laughs, "I should come out of retirement."

Several prominent players from the amateur era did just that in 1974 when a bizarre creation called World Team Tennis went into operation. Nothing had propelled the women toward profitable equality quite like WTT, although there is some question as to survival of this league, with its sixteen city teams comparable to baseball, football, and the other team sports. With the formation of WTT as the first coeducational team venture in sport, options for the men as well as the women increased. They could sign on with a team for a fixed salary for the May through August season and, if they wished, play tournaments the remainder of the year, most of which were now $50,000 minimum for women and $100,000 for men.

In signing a spectacular million-dollar (five-year) guaranteed contract with the Pittsburgh Triangles, Goolagong was likely the highest paid player in the league, making more than John Newcombe of Houston, Jimmy Connors of Baltimore, and her boss, player-coach Ken Rosewall of the Triangles. Since each engagement consisted of five one-set matches—men's singles and doubles, women's singles and doubles, and a mixed doubles—the women could readily measure their importance. Trish Bostrom of Boston exulted, "The feeling is great for a woman because her work on the team is just as meaningful as a man's. Our singles and doubles count the same as theirs, and we share the mixed. They can't win without us—or us without them."

Billie Jean, the first woman to boss men in a pro sport as player-coach at Philadelphia, ran her men ragged in arduous preseason training. Said salty old pro Fred Stolle of Mother Freedom's back-seat driving, "I didn't know if it would work out with Billie Jean, especially after some of the rough things she'd said about men. But it was all right. She pulled us together and made a family of us." Philadelphia made the best record over the season, but lost the playoff final to Denver, whose leading lady was Françoise Durr, that paragon of heterodoxy.

21

Nobody knows if WTT will last, but the opening season was bizarre fun. Some teams had coed dressing rooms. Husbands and wives were teammates and roommates on the road (Lesley and Bill Bowrey, Cynthia and Peter Doerner at Houston). A coach swapped his wife to another team (Clark Graebner, divorcing Carole Graebner, shipped her to Pittsburgh in exchange for a blonde named Laura DuPont). For the first time in pro sport—at least publicly—teammates became romantically involved (Kerry Melville and Raz Reid at Boston). A player dated a coach (Betty Grubb and Frank Froehling at Florida) and another player dated an owner (Julie Anthony and Dick Butera at Philadelphia). Women were active administrators (part-owners Betty Jones at Houston and Cathy Anderson at Golden Gate, promotions director Barbara Shotel at Philadelphia).

Offering a clearly defined season, a definite paycheck, and the chance to settle for that period in one city, WTT had attractive openings on the player rosters for family women. Donna Floyd Fales, last seen in 1967, found a baby-sitter for her three kids and went to work for Florida. The bartered bride, Carole Graebner, mother of two, who'd been a Forest Hills finalist in 1964, did the same. "Us more mature women can keep up," said Carole, "because the matches are only one set."

What a dizzying contrast to what faced the few women who occasionally tried to pioneer pro tennis before its time. Four of them were Sarah Palfrey Cooke and Pauline Betz in 1947, and Althea Gibson and Karol Fageros in 1959. Sarah Cooke (now Mrs. Jerome Danzig), national champion in 1941 and 1945, recalls, "Pauline Betz, who had won Wimbledon in 1946, and I were contemplating turning pro to play a tour against each other. There were no pro tournaments for women then, and very few for men. We sent letters to schools, colleges, and clubs asking if they'd be interested in having us play. As soon as the USLTA heard about it—we were just inquiring, mind you —they suspended us. That shows you how narrow-minded tennis officials were then.

"Nevertheless, the response to our letters was favorable, and we went on tour, playing for $200 or $300 here and there, frequently driving all night to get to the next place. But we were like kids getting paid for something we loved. It was fun. Later we toured Europe with Don Budge and Bobby Riggs, who were playing against each other. For that year we made about $10,000 apiece, which we thought was very good, but after expenses and taxes we'd only broken even."

One-nighters on basketball floors for usually uninterested customers constituted the professional life of Althea Gibson after she won Wimbledon and Forest Hills in 1958. "Karol Fageros and I signed on to tour with the Harlem Globetrotters," says Althea, now program director of the Valley View Racquet Club at Northvale, New Jersey. They were only part of the act, trimming for the basketball clowns, along with the jugglers and tap dancers. "We would open the show, playing on the basketball court. Karol and I played thirty-three matches between October of 1958 and April of 1959, and I won all but five of them." Fageros, better known for her frilly costumes and golden hairdos, was ranked 14th in the U.S. when they embraced professionalism. Gibson—on a nightly $800 guarantee—says she made over $100,000 on that tour, and later did play one tournament. "It was in Cleveland, 1960, six of us in it, and I beat Pauline Betz in the final. My manager tried to find out what's what with the gate receipts, and never could. Couldn't have been much anyway. Attendance was nothing. I got peanuts, maybe a couple of hundred dollars. There was nothing more to do playing pro tennis, so I tried the golf tour. Then teaching tennis, which I'm doing now."

Althea, a tall, strong woman who also pioneered socially by leaping the color barrier in American tennis, sighs, "Oh, the money I could have made playing today if I was in my prime. But you can't cry over spilt milk."

Evonne Goolagong, of course, is pleased that she's made so much money (if she's noticed), that she's become a personage, and that her sport is going places. But she is not as ecstatic as you might think. By that I mean the money doesn't really do anything for her. She leaves the accounting to proxy papa Vic Edwards and has few material desires beyond purchasing a house for her parents. ("After all," says Vic, "how many pairs of jeans can you wear?")

An absolutely converse feeling is expressed by Rosie Casals. "I like money. It's a symbol of how good I am. It's freedom. I like good cars and my house on the ocean, traveling first class and buying what I want. When I was a kid I couldn't afford a racket, couldn't afford tournament entry fees. Money was important. Now that I've got it," says Rosie, who earned $104,375 in prize money for 1973 and had a plush contract with Detroit of WTT in 1974, "I'm not going to pretend it's not important and that I don't enjoy it."

Casals, growing up in San Francisco, was probably no poorer than Goolagong in Barellan, but she felt her poverty more acutely. Evonne rolls with life's punches—perhaps this is her Aboriginal nature. This isn't to say she's a thorough I-don't-care girl. She would rather win than lose, eat and live well than not. But defeat never bothers her. I don't think economic hardship would either. She's so vague about finances that she'd never be able to tell you how much prize money is at stake in a tournament or what she's won. There might not be another player around who isn't conversant with a tournament's prize money structure. A competitor says of Evonne, "When you're that good and don't have to scrape, you don't have to pay attention." Still, no one would accuse Billie Jean of not paying attention.

The fact is Evonne's nature is so free and gay, trusting and fatalistic, undemanding and ingenuous that she often seems unreal. Traveling within sophisticated circles, she remains unsophisticated and fresh. Sometimes, so unaware of race and politics, and unconcerned with them, she can be maddening. Yes, she has said, "South Africa is one of my favorite places." And it is. The climate and people agree with her, and the police state aspects are not on view to her. She was uncomfortable over the furor that preceded her first visit to South Africa, but she believed in Vic Edwards and went unquestioningly. I would say she accomplished something, however small, making a tiny dent in apartheid as the first nonwhite to play tennis among whites. Some Aboriginal activists would not agree. One, an officer in an Australian government agency, told me, "It was an insult to her people to play for those racists. But living with the Edwardses has made Evonne more white than Aboriginal. The whole arrangement is paternalism at its worst."

Certainly the Edwardses, Vic and his jolly wife, Eva, have been paternalistic. Yet anyone spending time with them and Evonne in their Sydney home can't help but be impressed with them all as members of a loving family. She is a young woman who has been closely supervised: at first so that an exceptional talent could be refined, and later as a precious daughter in the Edwards family. Whatever you think of her upbringing, it hasn't diminished the charm that captivates wherever she plays. Her joy in the game and in life are so evident.

Can anyone, particularly such a well-publicized figure, be as casual as Evonne? So blithe? So insouciant? Is it an act, I've been asked.

Rosie Casals answers, "What you see is what there is with Evonne. Win or lose, the sun will come up tomorrow. Life will go on or it won't. She's as nice and pleasant as she seems, friendly but not familiar. She's happy. No brooding, no introspection. Her head is just there. No problems. She's just Evonne, that's all. Who can be like that? Nobody else I've run into in this life."

"I'm at a loss to explain what goes on in her head," says the person who knows her best, Vic Edwards. "Oh, she has bad moods with the good of course. It drives me up the wall to see her throw away matches she should win. But who knows where her mind goes when this happens? You accept. She's Evonne. Never been a player like her."

Never. I doubt she'll pile up records. She'll win most of her matches. There will be more major titles. But she harbors no obsession with winning. After losing that brilliant 1974 Forest Hills final to Billie Jean, she indicated that the loss had cut deeper than usual. "It will probably take me until tomorrow to forget it," Evonne said seriously.

I think of her as a South Seas princess dancing, a gazelle gliding —she is all grace and lyrical motion. The theme of her performances is "Let the Sunshine In."

The aging pros regard her as a spiritual throwback to them.

"Evonne radiates joy," says Sarah Palfrey Cooke Danzig. "You can tell she's playing for the sheer fun of it. Now that the big money is here, none of them would play for free. But Evonne would."

Others would, too. But would they grin at their own mistakes as Evonne does? Could they transmit the delight of the game and make the onlooker glad merely to be there looking at her?

Tennis has become a profession, a career, a better place for gamesplaying women to make their way. That's all right with Evonne Goolagong, but she is not interested in the particulars, the shoptalk, the players' labor union. For her the game remains the thing—the rhythm of the chase and the strike, the elation of the combat and movement that moves her and us. It is more than a game and a career. Tennis is Evonne's being, and it becomes a very special celebration of beauty and verve when she plays it.

Bud Collins
Boston, 1974

EVONNE!

Goolagong's the name—it's a grand old name, much older than the nation of my birth. Nearly as old, perhaps, as the Australian continent itself, a land once possessed by my people, who roamed it in freedom and dignity, who gave you names like Mooloolaba, Katoomba, Waukaringa, Queanbeyan, Gidgiegolambo, Mullumbimby, Goobal, Bli Bli, Cookardinia, Grong Grong, Yarrawonga, Wagga Wagga, Wulgumerang, Goondiwindi, and countless others. Now we are aliens in our own country. Another civilization has taken over, and we are second-class citizens. Aborigines. We've left our mark across the continent, and I've left mine across the world, but I grew up as a bushie—a country girl—in Barellan, Narrandera Shire, New South Wales, Australia. Four hundred miles southwest of Sydney, a short distance in the vastness of Australia, but a long way spiritually for me. I still go back, when I can, for a day or two, to fish for yabbies.

We used to go fishing for yabbies in the small, muddy ponds called dams outside of town. These dams—merely dimples dug out of the ground to catch rainwater for the sheep—were our swimming pools and fishing holes in the bush country, a flat, hot dry land fit only for wheat and sheep. A tennis champion had never grown there before.

Yabbies are eager. They're a kind of crayfish, and they'll claw hungrily at anything you throw for them. Put a piece of sausage on a string and you'll get a yabbie. I don't know if yabbies think beyond the next meal or wonder what it's like to rise above their little pond. But they do rise—if you're lucky—only to wind up in a pot of very hot water. Yabbies are delicious. We Goolagongs love them.

I was a little like a yabbie myself, happy in my home at the bottom, but curious about life above, eager to grab anything that might get me there.

The biggest pond in my life is Wimbledon, formally known as The Lawn Tennis Championships at the All England Lawn Tennis and Croquet Club in the London suburb of Wimbledon. Wimbledon: that one word means everything to a tennis player and has to tennis players everywhere for nearly a century, even though it doesn't appear on a trophy or in the formal title of the tournament. Wimbledon is a place, a tradition, a style, a business, a celebration, a dream, a prize. Moreover, Wimbledon is fun.

Few people knew about the tournament in 1877 when some blokes—women weren't welcome to compete until 1884—with lopsided rackets gathered amidst the greenery to entertain themselves by hitting a little ball over a net until one of them, Spencer W. Gore, had beaten all his opponents to win the first of The Lawn Tennis Championships. That was a tennis tournament; not the first tournament, but the first of note. Not the championship of London or England or Britain, but simply, and imperiously, The Lawn Tennis Championships, as if no other tournament mattered. To a lot of people, no other tournament does matter. If you win here, you are the world champion and that's that.

To some, tennis may be only a simple game of batting a ball over a net, but the devotion and attention Wimbledon gets make it important throughout the world. To me, though, it's still only a game.

I won't say I enjoyed playing on the dirt courts of Barellan as much as I do on the handsomely trimmed lawns of the All England Club, the clay of Rome, the cement of Johannesburg, or the gritty composition courts of Cincinnati. The game is exhilarating anywhere, but the people in the grandstand make the difference—customers, aficionados, tennis nuts. We play for the crowd as much as for ourselves, and when those seats are filled, we play our best. Since more people see me at Wimbledon—14,000 jammed into Centre Court, plus millions more watching the telly—and the English are such appreciative fans, that fortnight is the most important of my year.

Unfortunately, for some of the players the importance attached to Wimbledon turns the lovely big pond into a pot of hot water where they're boiled like groping yabbies. I know the feeling, but it left me after my first Wimbledon.

So here I was, the bushie, the brown-skinned descendant of wandering boomerang throwers, in my second Wimbledon at a very unlikely stage. It was Friday, July 2, 1971, the eleventh and next-to-last day of the tournament, and I was still playing. Ninety-six of us had started in the chase for the biggest prize, and now two of us were left: Margaret Court, who could have counted her major finals on her toes only if she were a centipede, and me, Margaret Court's number-one worshiper. Margaret won her first Wimbledon in 1963, when I was eleven. I think I must have been as pleased as she was. There's still a newspaper clipping of one of her triumphs on the wall of our kitchen in Barellan. I wanted Margaret to win every match and everything she went after.

Until today. This one I wanted for myself. I wasn't supposed to be here. At nineteen I had a chance to be the youngest champion since Karen Susman won at the same age nine years before. I was the youngest finalist since Billie Jean King, also nineteen, lost to Margaret eight years before. I'd outdistanced my No. 3 seeding, and I was way ahead of the timetable made up by my coach, Vic Edwards. He had predicted I'd win Wimbledon in 1974.

Centre Court, Wimbledon. The final. Prime ministers and princesses staring at me, as well as the people of three or four continents hooked into television. My heroine, Margaret, stood across the way, looking tall, strong, and not very charitable.

How did I get here? By chauffeur-driven limousine, in the Wimbledon custom. But not all the way from Barellan of course. The only way I could have gotten from the War Memorial Tennis Club in Barellan to Centre Court of the All England Lawn Tennis and Croquet Club in London was to fly on a racket.

I changed vehicles frequently. First there was the banged-up hand-me-down racket with cheap, withered, off-key strings that punged instead of pinged. Then came a new and better one. Then stacks of gleaming, tautly strung smashers supplied compliments of the manufacturer. And eventually a Dunlop Evonne Goolagong model with my picture on the throat.

The route was indirect, and it took a long, long time. Even at nineteen I had a lot of mileage on me, miles and miles of prowling a rectangular world of 1,053 square feet all over the world, corner to corner, baseline to net, side to side—my half of a tennis court.

My success seems to depend on the skill of my opponent, and I like it when she makes me run because that keeps my interest up. For me the most fun is catching up with and hitting a ball that looks impossible to reach. If there's not enough prodding from my opponent, if she's not challenging, the Goolagong fog descends and I vanish in a haze of inattention. The Goolagong form is still there, hacking away and losing points, but I'm on automatic pilot. My mind is off on an excursion somewhere, and I'm oblivious to the score. I'm going through the motions, but they aren't winning motions.

When this happens, my opponent cheers up. She begins to win, and she learns that the best way to beat me is to play miserably and lose the first set, thereby destroying my concentration, and, presto, do a turnaround and win the next two before the fog lifts.

When this happens, my fans groan, "not again"; my coach, Vic Edwards, tries to light two cigarettes at once; and most spectators nod knowingly, "Evonne's gone walkabout."

By this time my walkabout, which is nothing more than a loss of concentration, has become a characteristic widely celebrated by sports journalists.

Walkabout: fade away, retreat, withdraw, bug out, get away from it all. It can be physical or mental. Or both. In my case it's almost always mental. I've accepted the expression "walkabout" for my spells, but the word didn't come from me. It came from Mr. Edwards. Though I know he wasn't being condescending, it is an expression that irritates many Aborigines because it is the white man's word for an Aborigine trait, and because it is a word that is frequently used derisively to mean shiftless or purposeless.

Originally the trait of walking about was the essence of Aborigine life. It was anything but shiftless. Aborigines were keen, resourceful people who understood nature, migrating with the seasons, always moving to the most favorable living conditions. When the food and good weather were exhausted, they got out and walked to more hospitable territory. Life was hard, but they stayed ahead of the game. Maybe it was always match point against them, but they kept beating it—until whites arrived in Australia. From that point it was downhill for the Aborigine, as it was for the American Indian.

The Aborigine population was about 350,000 when an Englishman, Captain James Cook, appeared as Australia's first tourist of 1770. Today the Aborigine population is 125,000. The white man's brutality wiped out thousands of free, vigorous people, relegating the rest to a life of subservience and poverty. The Aborigines are outcasts in their own country, a country that has become extremely prosperous.

Things are changing for the better: education and opportunity for Aborigines are improving, but there's a long way to go. When you're blanketed by a new civilization and are expected to conform to that civilization—yet given no chance to advance yourself in it or really be a part of it—it's easy to fall into despair. You walk away from it or close your mind. We're a gentle people. We'd rather switch off than fight. If the pressure of the white man's world becomes too heavy, we go walkabout.

It's good copy, a colorful expression, and I don't mind it a bit. But it grates on a lot of Aborigines because of its background. They take it as part of the white put-down of the Aborigine. I can understand both sides because I'm from both sides.

33

On that improbable July afternoon when I faced Margaret Court on Centre Court for the tennis championship of the world, also known as The Lawn Tennis Championship, I did not go walkabout. I ran about having a glorious time, giving the sports commentators someone new to talk about; suddenly Goolagong was a household name. But it always was, if yours was an Aborigine household in the bush.

I chose tennis early by grabbing for a ball like a mindless yabbie. My Dad had bought a secondhand Chevy and discovered on the floor several grimy tennis balls—apparently one of the car's previous owners had been a player. Dad never knew or cared. It could have been better—he might have found some money. And it could have been worse—there might have been some tarantulas living under the seat. For me it was perfect. Dad gave me a ball, and I stopped crying. Mum was impressed: a tennis ball had soothed her cranky baby, Evonne.

Mum says, "Evonne was twelve months old when we came across those balls, and they made her real happy. They was like a rattle for her. Them and chewing gum. Every time we'd go into Griffith I'd get her a ball for seven pence and some gum. She didn't have any teeth, but she'd chew a whole pack at one time. She'd sit in her pram with her baldy head, playing with a ball and chewing all day, happy as anything.

"I'd worry about her because she didn't walk for a long time. She'd run around like a dog on her hands and knees and her hands got real hard. Then one day, when she was two, she just started walking."

But not walking about, just walking around the neighborhood, and always with a tennis ball. Three years later, they built the War Memorial Tennis Club in Barellan and gave us a place to play. After all, you can't become a champion merely by fondling a ball, although Rod Laver says he strengthened his incredibly strong left wrist by squeezing a tennis ball as a boy. Maybe I was preparing my wrist for tennis without knowing it, but you still have to learn to hit the ball.

That rusting Chevy was my treasure trove, but, in a way, it was nearly the end of me before I ever swung a racket. I enjoyed crawling

34

around the car, watching Dad when he tinkered with it, and one day, I'm told, I was fascinated by his siphoning petrol out of the tank with a hose. He'd get it started flowing by sucking on the hose. I thought he was drinking whatever it was, and later, when he was doing something else, I crawled over to the hose to take a drink. I began sucking away as though I had a straw in lemonade. Nothing like a little high-test to get you going—to the hospital. I've heard Americans call gin-and-tonic a Blue Sunoco, and I've heard the expression "getting gassed," but this was a ridiculous way to get tanked up.

I must have made an awful noise, and luckily Mum heard me. "Evonne turned purple," Mum says. "I thought she'd swallowed a nut. She was choking and crying. I didn't know what she'd done, but I knew it was bad. Her dad had the car apart so we couldn't drive. I picked her up and ran to the main road (about 300 yards) and hailed a car. We got a ride to the hospital in Griffith (thirty-three miles), and they pumped her stomach. The doctor said we just made it in time. What a scare she gave us."

We were poor, but we Goolagong kids didn't know it. ("Poor but happy," is what Mum says, and that's my recollection.) Our house was the worst in town. I can see that now when I go back. We might not have had some things the other kids had, like bikes and nice clothes, but everybody seemed pretty much the same in Barellan.

Now I'm aware of my uniqueness as the only Aborigine in tennis, but it didn't occur to us Goolagong kids to feel different, even though we were the town's only family of "dark people," as my mother calls Aborigines. My father, an itinerant sheep-shearer, had come to Barellan when I was about two because there was good opportunity for him in the area.

Our old house is still there on Bendee Street, an abandoned tin shack with scruffy, ink-blotched linoleum floors. Faded lettering over the front door identifies the structure as the office of the Barellan *Leader,* a newspaper that has gone the way of too many newspapers —down the drain. I'm not suggesting the Barellan *Leader* (whose circulation might have been 1,000) was top class, but I'm sorry it didn't last long enough to run my picture when I won Wimbledon.

Normally you can expect to see your picture in your hometown newspaper when you win a world title, unless your hometown isn't big enough to have a paper. The news was in the Temora *Leader,* the Wagga Wagga *Daily Advertiser,* and the Murrumbidgee *Irrigator*— papers that cover the Barellan area.

The Barellan *Leader* had folded before we got there in 1953, but they left the printing press behind. Some kids have jungle gyms, but we had a newspaper press to climb on and lead slugs to play with, the thin slabs of type (with the printing on backwards) that make up a newspaper column. There were five of us kids in Ken and Melinda Goolagong's family during most of the time I was growing up in Barellan, with three yet to come. I was born in 1951, third oldest. Barbara is five years older and Larry two years older. Two years after me Kevin was born, then Gail two years later. They're the ones I know best. We were together before I left home for good at thirteen, when I realized I had to live in Sydney if I was going to have a real go at tennis. Janelle, eight years younger than me, was a baby when I left and so were Ian and Martin, who are ten and twelve years younger.

Mum, an only child herself, born in the same mud hut as her mother before her, was pregnant ten times, starting at sixteen. She lost two through miscarriages, but she wouldn't have minded having eight more. I haven't noticed her giving tennis balls to any of her grand-children, though. Maybe she reckons that was a bad influence. "You're slow, Evonne," she needles me. "No kids yet at your age. I had four by then."

There was plenty for me to do in Barellan, in the days before I'd ever seen an airplane. It was a crowded metropolis of 900 people in those days, but today Barellan is disappearing. The biggest market has closed, along with several other businesses. Sadly, the most romantic name in Barellan commerce—the Vienna Café—has shut down, and nothing lies behind its colorful cutglass nameplate and clouded win-dows. As you walk down Yapunyah Street, the principal boulevard of Barellan (and just about the only one that's paved), you can't miss the Vienna Café. Unless you're a fast walker, in which case you might miss the town altogether.

As long as the surrounding wheat and sheep properties continue to thrive, however, something will remain of Barellan. Trains go through twice a week to pick up wheat from the silos and the storehouse called the Bulkhead. Two buildings are sure to last: the Commercial Hotel and the War Memorial Club, where the beer flows to irrigate the men who look after the soil and livestock. If the crops and animals go dry, that is a natural calamity accepted by the cockies (the men who raise wheat and sheep). But if they go dry, that is a tragedy no one accepts. Life without beer isn't worth living out there.

It's treasonous, but I don't happen to like beer. The only other Australian I know of who doesn't drink beer is a tennis player named Bob Hewitt. He lives in South Africa now, and I'm afraid to ask if he was deported.

An old friend calls Barellan "Peyton Place with flies," one of those places everybody knows everything everybody else is doing. As an adult I wouldn't like that, but when you're a kid you don't think much about privacy or the need for anonymity. I feel that need most during Wimbledon time in London where the tennis fans are so keen. Sometimes it's impossible for me to walk around the grounds without being mobbed. I guess that's how a pop star feels all the time. It's enjoyable at first, but sometimes in one of those crushes I think: Wouldn't it be nice to be chasing rabbits back in Barellan.

Rabbit stew was one of my favorite foods. We were always eating stews with everything in them. It was Mum's specialty and a good way to feed a lot of people cheaply. My brothers Larry and Kevin and I and the dogs were always after rabbits. The boys had air guns and slingshots they used to get rabbits and sometimes birds. Very rarely would we see a kangaroo. No wombats, koalas, or platypuses either.

There's a big bird in the country called a galah, gray with red markings. A galah dips and climbs and darts about erratically, a nutty old bird that flew right into the Australian language: "Crazy as a galah" is quite a common remark. Sometimes the boys would knock one down with a wing shot and tame it. You can teach a galah to talk, in the same way as a parrot. Occasionally we'd catch a goanna, a big lizard. My Aunt Ethel cooks them beautifully. Tender as chicken, but better.

We'd add to the menu by finding huge swan eggs and catching yabbies and other fish. Fishing is my favorite form of relaxation. Most of my experience has been in country rivers and dams, but I did make an amusing score in the ocean off Sydney recently. A couple of my friends took me out on a cruiser, determined to teach me the finer points of fishing with rod and reel. The equipment was the best, and they seemed expert at using it. I caught on to the idea, but the rods and reels didn't appeal to me. I said I'd watch. They fished for a long time. Nothing. Finally, I said, "Let me show you how we do it in the country—the good, old-fashioned way." I took a handline, baited it, and threw it over the side. It wasn't long before I'd pulled in two big bass. They were fairly good sports about it—they didn't push me overboard.

I competed with boys for a long time. Billie Jean King played football with the neighborhood boys in Long Beach, California, until her mother pulled her off the street and told her to find a more feminine game. When I was eight or nine, I played rugby with the boys. I loved to run with the ball and to tackle. I played cricket and soccer, too, all this before I became really immersed in tennis.

And I ran. Speed has been a prime factor in my tennis, as it has been in Billie Jean's. With Margaret Court it's power and reach. Running makes me feel good and free; it's the best part of any sport. Peter Wilson, who has written on tennis (and every other game) for nearly a half-century for the London *Mirror*, believes, "There are only two natural sports: running and fighting. The rest are contrived."

I guess you could trace the beginning of my professional career back to running, to the age of nine when I collected about a dollar for winning a variety of races at our annual athletics day at school. The winner got sixpence a race (about ten cents), and I entered everything there was including the three-legged race.

We were outdoor kids all the way. There was only one indoor

38

game, pigeon hunting in the grain silos. The silos, six cement cylinders side by side, tower a hundred feet above Barellan, the tallest structures in town. Architectural masterpieces—if you like towering sewer pipes. Pigeons live in the wooden housing at the top, and when the silos were empty we'd climb the ladders inside to get up there. Rickety planks bridged canyons twenty-five feet across. We'd do a sort of tightrope-balancing act along the planks, snatching at pigeons, disdainful of the height. I gasp and shake my head every time I think of it now. I wouldn't even climb those ladders today, much less walk the planks.

You're never far from an open field in the country. There is endless room to play. I'm a city person now, but I can't imagine being raised in a city. A kid in the country has so much to do, but there's so little opportunity when the kid grows up. That's why people leave Barellan. Our whole family might have left, by popular request, after one of our escapades. My brothers and I had found some matches and were playing with them in a wheat field. Ripe wheat burns easily. Suddenly there was a fire, a brief but terrifying moment of smoke and flames, and a few minutes of panic and fear before we managed to stamp it out. It's very bad form to burn up the leading product of the town you live in. I can't remember what we told Mum, but it wasn't a very believable story, and we only told her the truth years later. Fortunately for the Goolagongs, we put out that fire.

Some of my best friends are white.

Without them there'd have been no tennis, no tournaments, no discovering and refining this talent I have for pursuing and pummeling a ball. It is not a talent that necessarily enriches mankind, but entertainment does have a value. It enhances life. Neither winning nor losing means as much to me as knowing the crowd has enjoyed my match. Some players feel that winning is everything and that losing is a disaster. Not me. I want the spectators to take home a good memory. If I had lost my 1972 Wimbledon semifinal to Chris Evert in three sets instead of winning in three, I would have been disappointed, but not displeased or angry. Because of the occasion, the

39

tension, the fight we both displayed, and our shotmaking, it will rank as one of the memorable matches. I was told that it was an emotionally draining experience for the viewers. Playing a part in a gripping sporting drama is all I can ask.

My career has been relatively short. I can't envision it ending, and I hope it won't for a long while, although I realize in sport the end can come abruptly. When it does, I'll be glad for all I've had.

There would have been no beginning if Bill Kurtzman hadn't taken a liking to me, and no career as such if Vic Edwards hadn't seen something in me that made a believer of him. Nothing would have happened if those two men hadn't met, become acquainted, and eventually cooperated in establishing me in Sydney.

Mr. Kurtzman was a retired grazier, fifty-eight, who had come in off the property to live in Barellan in 1953. He said he remembered first seeing me the next year, when I was three. I don't remember that. But I do remember when they built the War Memorial Tennis Club near our house in 1956. I hung around there watching my older sister and brother play.

Mr. Kurtzman had played tennis when he was younger, and he thought Barellan should have a club. There were a couple of courts in town, but nothing organized. Then Mr. Kurtzman began talking up interest and led a subscription drive. With those donations and the help of the local veterans' club, the Returned Servicemen's League, the tidy little tennis club was constructed. Four red loam courts with floodlights, well fenced, and adjoined by a small brick clubhouse. Wimbledon it is not—although the roses rival Wimbledon's—and yet I doubt that any community in the world of fewer than 1,000 population has a tennis club as nice.

Every town and city in Australia has an RSL Club where food, drink, entertainment, and recreation are cheap. Anybody can join. They're supported mainly by the bars and slot machines, called poker machines. A place like Barellan revolves around the War Memorial Club, which subsidizes the lawn bowling and tennis clubs. Thus an annual tennis membership is a staggering four dollars. The barroom is the hub of the entire farming community, the social and business center, the meeting place where Mr. Kurtzman called a group of leading citizens together to ask if they would join in sponsorship of my assault on Sydney and the world of big tennis. From this meeting came a pledge of weekly support of six dollars, and I was on my way.

That was quite a while after Mr. Kurtzman and I met. I was just a face peering through the tennis club fence when he first noticed me, according to Mrs. Kurtzman. I was no longer squeezing tennis balls in my pram but knocking them around with a borrowed racket against the cinder block wall of a vacant building near our house.

My luck lies principally in two names: Kurtzman and Edwards. Mr. Kurtzman took an interest in me and started me. Mr. Edwards followed through, refining the tennis-playing Goolagong. But of course he and his wife, Eva, did much more. They took me into their home, raised me as one of their daughters, and made me part of a lively and loving family, without disturbing the bond between me and my real family.

Everyone has to leave home, to live their life wherever they must to do what they have to do. I left earlier than most—at thirteen for good—but I wasn't actually leaving. I was transferring from the warmth of one home to the warmth of another. I didn't know that when I moved, though. I was nervous and frightened, uncertain about the Edwardses and living with people who would be very different. I didn't want to leave my family, but I couldn't get anywhere in tennis unless I moved on.

Wimbledon was out there somewhere. I discovered it in a comic book, not from a sports page or a telecast, the usual source of such information. I'd read a comic book about a young girl with mean parents who runs away from home and is taken in by a wealthy woman. The woman teaches the girl to play tennis, and the girl grows up to win Wimbledon. I can still see the last panels, the drawings of the girl on Centre Court with that great crowd around her.

That cartoonist's vision may have been a rough outline of my career, but very rough. My parents weren't mean, and I didn't run away. But I was taken in and taught tennis. I did win Wimbledon.

41

Victor Allan Edwards has been called my Professor Higgins, my Svengali, my surrogate father. These comments have not necessarily been complimentary.

He has been all of these to me, and I cannot compliment him enough. I was a pet project who became a prize exhibit, a discovery who became a champion, a plane ticket around the world who became a daughter and sister in his family. You will notice that I don't call my foster parents Mum and Dad or Eva and Vic. I call them Mr. and Mrs. Edwards and probably always will. Somehow it wouldn't seem right to say Mum and Dad because those names will always belong to my real parents, who are in Barellan.

Mister and Missis, usually terms of respect, are now expressions of affection to me when I use them for the Edwardses. I can understand why some people may consider me slightly outside the Edwards family when they hear me say Mr. Edwards to Vic. That doesn't worry us. The family is too close to be disturbed by things like that, and Mr. Edwards is too strong to be bothered by any criticism of our relationship.

It was a brief moment of hurt feelings some years ago that assured me I was one of the family. The Edwardses' oldest (of five) daughters had come to Sydney to visit. Robin Edwards Wride lives with her husband and six children on the other side of the country, in Perth, and I'd never met her. She came into the living room, and everybody gathered about her—everybody but me. I stood back, waiting to be introduced. I kept standing there, uncomfortable, and still nobody offered to introduce us. Nobody was paying any attention to me until Robin said, "Hey, this must be Evonne. Aren't I going to meet her? What's wrong with you people? No manners?"

Mrs. Edwards began to laugh her loud, marvelous laugh. " 'S' truth!" she shrieked, her "for-heaven's-sake" expression. "Never thought to introduce you to a member of your own family, Robin, but of course Evonne's come since you left. Well, it's time you met."

My left-out feeling vanished. We were all laughing and hugging, and I knew I belonged to this tribe.

Vic Edwards calls us his "harem": five natural daughters plus me, his wife, Eva, and the matriarch, his mother, May Edwards, a sturdy, remarkable Englishwoman we call Gran, who is amazingly enthusiastic and lucid into her nineties. My Wimbledon victory of 1971 occurred within a couple of days of Gran's eighty-eighth birthday. In 1920 she had sat in Centre Court watching Suzanne Lenglen winning the championship for a first time. Fifty-one years later she watched me on television and told me over the transoceanic phone, "Evonne, you were as graceful and good as Suzanne. That's the best birthday present anyone has ever given me."

Part of my luck was the failure of Gran's husband, Herbert Edwards, to use the steamship tickets he had purchased for their return to England. He'd been enticed to Australia just after World War I by an offer to supervise construction of the White City sporting grounds in Sydney since he was an expert at building football, tennis and cricket grounds. Herbert Edwards was one of the first to earn his living as a tennis instructor. He came from a section of London called Cricklewood, where Vic was born in 1909. The family spent some time in the Netherlands where Herbert taught prior to World War I.

It was a good combination, building and teaching, and Australia, a relatively new society with a strong interest in sport, seemed ripe for the Edwards approach. Australia had been something of a tennis power, winning the Davis Cup five times before World War I, largely through the exploits of two gifted men, Norman Brookes, an Australian, and Tony Wilding, a New Zealander. In fact, the team went under the banner of Australasia to include both countries. (New Zealand has had its own national team since 1924.) Teaching pros are numerous throughout the world today, but at the height of Brookes's and Wilding's success, there wasn't a single professional coach on the Australian continent. Herbert Edwards was the first. His son Vic carries on his father's work at the Victor A. Edwards Tennis School in Roseville, a peaceful Sydney suburb on the north side of the harbor.

For some reason, Herbert Edwards's appointment to build White City fell through, although somebody else did the job, and White City is a renowned name throughout the tennis world. So he decided to take his family back to England. The tickets were bought, but they never got on the boat. "I guess we were growing fonder of Australia all the time, the climate, the opportunities," says Gran.

"In 1925 we found this house in Duntroon Road, and Vic said, 'Mum, this is the place for us.' He was right. It was lovely, almost like the country. Only two houses on the street, and plenty of room for tennis courts. We were cut off from Sydney by the harbor. The bridge wouldn't be built for almost a decade. But there was a train and a ferry, not too difficult a journey. I've never been back to England, and I wouldn't care to go now. My friends are all dead, and this is my home."

It came to be my home, too, although we actually live around the corner. How many hours did I spend on the sandy loam courts of the Victor A. Edwards Tennis School? I wouldn't have any idea, but that's where the transformation of the bushie and her suspect strokes began.

The house is called Killarney, a one-story brick with the typical tile roof. Wrought iron tennis rackets adorn the front fence, and the school pennant inscribed VAETS stretches from the flagpole. In back, just beyond the huge laurel tree that dominates the grounds are six courts, a bangboard, and various teaching devices like a crossbar with balls on strings hanging from it. You can bash away at those balls without having to chase them or worry about knocking one over a fence.

Gran lives in her section of the house. The rest is devoted to offices for Mr. Edwards and his staff, administrators and instructors. This is the campus, the grounds, of the Victor A. Edwards Tennis School. VAETS is a school in every sense, the first of its kind, a school of hard knocks with a tennis racket—although accurate knocks are usually better than hard ones. There's even a school crest—crossed rackets—and motto—Veni Cognovi Vici—"I came, I learned, I conquered": Victor Edwards's variation on a theme by Caesar. I went through the school just like thousands of other pupils—some champions, the rest trained to hit the ball properly so they can have fun playing socially and in club competitions for the rest of their lives.

44

In the course of a week about 4,000 pupils attend VAETS, taking group lessons at a wide variety of locations, including the home campus on Duntroon Road. The Edwards system of mass instruction was formulated by Herbert Edwards, refined and institutionalized by Vic, and has been copied by coaches all over the world. Mr. Edwards's assistants conduct classes at courts all over Sydney while he oversees the entire operation. Each student is graded and moved along to a more advanced class whenever improvement warrants. In teaching the stroke-production drills, an instructor can keep fifteen students busy on one court.

Mr. Edwards is extremely organized. Every portion of the lesson is outlined and posted beforehand; every minute is occupied. No time to stand around, gawking and wondering. They keep you swinging, whether or not a ball is actually involved.

During the week his instructors appear at high schools and colleges to give mass lessons to the student bodies. Each pupil there is graded, too. Careful reports are made by the instructors to Mr. Edwards on the progress of these thousands of enrollees at VAETS. These reports are sent to him even when he's overseas, touring the tennis circuit with me. He's as thorough and meticulous as an American football coach in his organization and administration.

It was Mr. Edwards's reputation for group instruction that brought him into contact with Mr. Kurtzman. One of the features of VAETS is the country schools set up for one week in the rural areas of New South Wales. Every year during the August holidays, Mr. Edwards sends teams of coaches to operate teaching programs in eleven or twelve country centers, such as Gondegai, Young, and Cowra. This gives kids from the bush an opportunity for first-rate instruction, a chance to learn a game that will be a social focal point for country families who drive miles to play at courts in small towns. Almost every town has a court or two.

These country schools of VAETS are very close to Mr. Edwards. He spent much of his young manhood on the land as a jackeroo—the Australian equivalent of a cowboy—and he realizes what tennis can mean to enrich the lives of country people. He also is aware that some

45

of Australia's greatest players have sprouted from the bush, from places that even other Australians had never heard of—Rod Laver from Langdale, Roy Emerson from Blackbutt, Mal Anderson from Theodore, Tony Roche from Tarcutta, Jan Lehane O'Neill from Grenfell. Like any coach, Mr. Edwards is always keen to find a player with championship potential.

With Barellan's War Memorial Club built, Mr. Kurtzman contacted Mr. Edwards with the thought that my town would be a good place for a country school. Would Mr. Edwards consider it? Mr. Kurtzman didn't have me or anyone else in particular in mind as star pupil. Now that he had the courts, he wanted all the kids of the area to have a chance to learn the fundamentals of the game.

Mr. Edwards went to Barellan to meet Mr. Kurtzman, look the place over, and stipulate that if eighty youngsters would pay the tuition, they could have a school. Our club paid mine, which seemed a lot, but by American standards of tennis coaching was nothing: six dollars.

Colin Swan and Faith Martin were assigned to the Barellan School, and I suppose it was a case of mutual shock for us and them. Tennis for us had been just trying to hit a ball over a net the best we could. Faith and Colin now made it known that there was a better way —a right way—and they set about teaching us in a very organized manner. In six days we got about the same amount of instruction the city kids get in a term of thirteen Saturdays. There was no break between classes. We went at it solid, and after the week we felt we'd really come along.

Repetition is the heart of learning tennis—hitting shots over and over until they become second nature, thousands and thousands of shots. We started with The Drill, the backbone of the Edwards system. We got so we could do The Drill with military precision, and I think maybe Mr. Edwards got the idea from the manual of arms when he was in the army. We could also do any part of it without thinking, as the instructor ordered.

The Drill is made up of the component parts of a stroke: ready position stance, backswing, impact-making swing, creating spin (if desired, slice or topspin), follow-through. You go through it again and again, without a ball, so that your footwork, balance, and swing are set in your mind before you try to hit a ball. Part of each graduation ceremony at VAETS is devoted to The Drill, as though it were a dress parade. A photo on the wall of Mr. Edwards's office shows his daughter Jenifer, at age six, standing on a platform at White City Stadium leading 500 children in The Drill.

Your two opponents—the player on the other side of the net and the ball—seldom cooperate in allowing you to hit a shot under the ideal conditions of The Drill. The Drill simply prepares you with the fundamental stroke, which must be adjusted to the speed and height of the ball, to the bounce and the spin. That's why you have to hit thousands of balls. Thousands? More like millions if you're thinking about playing tennis really well. That's how you groove a stroke and gain confidence in it, so that you can swing away without thinking about it regardless of the score.

It becomes a bit mindless and mechanical, but as long as a human being is involved that can't happen altogether. "Relax and hit for the lines" is the advice Harry Hopman used to give such players as Ken Rosewall, Rod Laver, Roy Emerson, and John Newcombe, whom he captained on Australia's Davis Cup team. It doesn't sound like much of a revelation. "But," said Fred Stolle after winning the critical singles over Dennis Ralston in Australia's 1964 cup-winning triumph over the U.S., "what Hop wanted was for you to hit out just as you'd done in practice and forget about the score. The thing is, if you'd practiced hard enough and grooved your strokes it would work for you."

The ordinary player doesn't have that kind of background and so can't forget the score and hit with that kind of confidence. But that's what Mr. Edwards intended to do with me, once he'd taken me under his wing. He makes sure I spend enough time on the court, hitting strokes over and over so that I can produce them automatically. If I don't, right back to the practice court we go.

It's the only way. You have to practice with purpose; it doesn't do much good to hit the ball the wrong way over and over. When

47

things aren't going well, or I'm returning to competition after a layoff, Mr. Edwards is on the court with me, watching my strokes carefully. He used to hit with me himself. Now he supervises while someone else does the hitting.

There were three Goolagongs in the school at Barellan. My older sister and brother, Barbara and Larry, along with me. Mr. Edwards thinks Barbara might have been better than me and that Larry could have been quite good. Neither was as interested, although Barbara, who went into nursing, got married, and is raising a family, still plays at a club level in Narrandera, not far from Barellan.

"You could tell the Goolagongs all right," says Mrs. Martin. "They stood out not only because they were darker than the rest of the kids, but also for their ability and appearance. They had only one tennis outfit apiece, but Mrs. Goolagong would see to it those clothes were spotless. She boiled them every night in a copper pot and dried them by the fire."

I still take some clothes home for Mum to wash when I visit Barellan. I don't feel they're really clean until she boils them.

Mrs. Martin and Mr. Swan continue to conduct the Barellan school every year during the August holidays, and by this time they've gotten over the shock. Unless you're used to a country town like that, anything more than a day can seem a pretty long visit. The one hotel, according to some of the guests, would make the Black Hole of Calcutta seem like a Holiday Inn. The beds are as soft as granite, and Mr. Swan says his room has had the same broken window for thirteen years. He also says he's grown kind of fond of the place and has become accustomed to the broad range of breakfast treats: baked beans on toast and spaghetti on toast. The bread is toasted on the gas burners that heat the kitchen.

In Australia a hotel exists principally to cater to the needs of a thirsty populace. You stay at a motel, and you drink at a hotel. Every town has a hotel. The smallest don't have motels. The law states that the hotelkeeper must have some rooms available for rent. That's about all those rooms are—available.

There are small hotels everywhere in the bush. Ranjit Chopra, a young Indian who came to Australia to play some of our smaller tournaments, will never forget the hotel in Warren. Uncle Stan Edwards (Vic's brother, who is also a professional coach) was with Ranjit. Uncle Stan had been all through the country, but it was new to Ranjit, and a little disturbing. One morning Ranjit got up and was looking for what we call the dunny—the toilet. "Oh, it'll be out behind the hotel somewhere, Ranjit," Uncle Stan said. Ranjit finally found it, a hole hidden in an impenetrable horde of flies. Impossible. He went looking for the hotelkeeper to complain, "How can I use that toilet?"

"Ah, that's easy, mate," replied the boss, "you just wait till noon, and them flies'll all be in the dining room."

But those who like the country like it very much. Mr. Edwards is one who would have preferred to spend his life out there, and he enjoys his country schools. Luckily Mrs. Martin and Mr. Swan don't mind it. Lucky for me, because they're the ones who put me on the way to Sydney. They were the first people who were really knowledgeable about tennis to see me play and to have an idea that I might get somewhere.

"The first thing we noticed was the way Evonne moved. She was a natural athlete," says Mrs. Martin. "It was what we expected from a member of that family after we'd had Barbara and Larry in the school. But Evonne was something a little special.

"Colin and I didn't take a look at her and say, 'There's a Wimbledon champion!' Nothing that dramatic. We just noted she was quick and eager to learn, had fine reflexes and that wonderful movement.

"It went into the reports to the boss—Vic—that we make on all the schools and pupils. I suppose we mentioned her to him, but you don't go overboard on a nine year old after one week of a school. You couldn't forget her either, though. Colin and I wondered if she'd be there when we came back for the school the next year. You never know if a child will maintain the interest year to year. And with the Goolagongs being Aboriginals, you wouldn't count on their not moving somewhere else.

"The next year, though," Mrs. Martin says, "we really got carried away by Evonne. She was back in the school, and she'd improved so much. Col and I got so carried away that we phoned the boss, who was at another school about 700 miles away. Col told him, 'Boss, you've got to see this little Aboriginal girl. She's the best prospect we've ever seen.'

"I don't think the boss approved of phoning that distance to rave about a ten year old. He asked Col to talk to me and he said, 'Are you sure? Are you both sure?'

" 'Quite sure.'

" 'All right, I'll fly up. It better be worth it.'

"He did, and right away he agreed with us. But so what? What was to be done for or about an admittedly talented, but poor, very poor, kid in Barellan. An Aboriginal at that. There hadn't ever been any Aboriginals in tennis.

"So she'd keep coming to our school every year, and Bill Kurtzman would continue taking her around to the small country tournaments—Cootamundra, Leeton, Yanco, Wagga Wagga, Tumut, West Wyalong. Nobody was going to become a champion out of that. The boss had to take her to Sydney. Somebody had to.

"I think I got pretty emotional about it," Mrs. Martin recalls. She was determined that I get a chance, even though she knew just about everybody would be against it. She realized what most people said about Aborigines—that we couldn't stick to anything long enough to make a success of it, and also that country children don't as a rule like to leave home. Mrs. Martin told the boss that a champ was a champ, regardless of color.

By this time it was also in Mr. Kurtzman's mind that I should have a chance to see what I could do in better competition. He'd always been a booster. He'd given me my first new racket, and he was buoyed by what Mrs. Martin and Mr. Swan said about me. They'd told him how Mr. and Mrs. Edwards had taken in another country girl, Jan Lehane from Grenfell, to live with them during the 1950s. Jan grew up with the older Edwards girls, Robin, Vicki, and Jann, and became a high-ranking Australian player, good enough to travel the international circuit. In 1961 she won the Italian doubles with Lesley

Turner and reached the Wimbledon doubles final with Margaret Court, where they lost to Billie Jean King and Karen Susman.

This gave Mr. Kurtzman an opening to ask Mr. Edwards if I couldn't do the same. Jan Lehane had obviously been a different case. Her parents could pay for her upkeep in Sydney, and she was white. She fit right into the Edwards household. But would I? Would Mr. and Mrs. Edwards even be interested?

Mr. Edwards was intrigued by the idea, but he's a man who thinks ahead and considers all the possibilities. He talked about it with Mr. Kurtzman for a long time and pointed out the difficulties not only of taking a youngster away from home into a new environment but also of removing her from her family.

Even if Mrs. Edwards approved, he told Mr. Kurtzman, it would have to be done in easy stages. He checked with Mrs. Edwards, and they decided to invite me to Sydney for a three-week school holiday, to play the age-group tournaments always held in Sydney at that time. Then they could see how I'd get along with the girls at home, Patricia, a year younger than me, and Jenifer, a year older, and how I'd stand being away from my own family.

"Evonne was shy and quiet at first, but," remembers Mrs. Edwards, "from the first she was one of us. The girls fell for her— although they didn't know quite what to expect when we told them a little Aboriginal girl was coming to visit."

Trisha wondered, "How'll we know who she is when she gets off the plane?"

"She'll have a tennis racket, dear," said Mrs. Edwards.

But I found out the girls thought I'd be wearing a loincloth and carrying a spear. That's what came to their minds when they heard the Aborigine was coming to town.

You'd be amazed the image that word brings to some people's minds. Sometimes I go along with it, and do a put-on of my own. "Ah, yes," I say, "you should see me throw a boomerang. All my people are experts at it." I've never thrown one in my life.

That boomeranged on me at a tournament in New Zealand where one of the officials overheard me. Between matches I was startled to hear my name over the loudspeaker: ". . . and now we're pleased to present a demonstration of the ancient art of boomerang throwing by Miss Evonne Goolagong, one of our competitors. We have some fine authentic boomerangs . . . will Miss Goolagong please come down here and show us how it's done?"

I had to confess that it might be a Goolagong specialty, but not in my branch of the family.

I don't think I felt any different on the morning of that Wimbledon final than on any other day of a tennis tournament. Maybe I was more relaxed because I'd gone beyond my No. 3 seeding. I'd accomplished more than anybody expected, and so if I lost the final to Margaret it would only back up the wisdom of the London bookmakers. I'd been 1 to 15 before the tournament began, and Margaret was still favored 8 to 5 on the morning of the match. The fact that bookmakers handle Wimbledon business and will give you a price on any player in the tournament tells you something about the enthusiasm of the English for Wimbledon.

London is the only place in the world where the bookies care a hoot about tennis, although American bookies got into the game for the first time when Bobby Riggs played Billie Jean King late in 1973, but that was illegal. In Britain and at home in Australia bookmaking is an honorable occupation. Riggs was the 5 to 2 favorite and lost thousands in numerous head-to-head bets when Billie Jean went at him like Joan of Arc.

Riggs had better luck with London bookies in 1939, winning nearly $100,000 betting on himself—when he was an amateur! He went into a bookmaker's shop, put down £100 (the predevaluation pound was worth a little over four dollars), and said he wanted it across the board on the singles, doubles, and mixed on Robert L. Riggs. What prices would they give him?

The reply was: 3 to 1 on the singles, 6 to 1 on the doubles, and 12 to 1 on the mixed doubles. He had to win all three to collect, an extraordinarily rare achievement that has been matched by a man only once since then. Bobby did it, with help from Elwood Cooke in the doubles and Alice Marble in the mixed doubles. Says Bobby, "I just let it sit in a London bank gathering interest during the war." That chunk is presumably the basis of his fortune.

Unfortunately for Bobby, his 1939 head couldn't offset his 1973 legs and reflexes when he played Billie Jean in the Astrodome, although four months earlier at Ramona, California, he became the temporary king of mixed singles by badly beating Margaret Court.

Margaret got nervous and she froze. The ballyhoo, the Riggs psych, the strange setting—a hastily built court at a housing development—got to her. She wasn't the Margaret Court I'd grown up admiring and idolizing. Most of the times I've played Margaret I've felt a little funny, as if I shouldn't really be on the same court with the woman I've looked up to, and most of the time she's beaten me.

I'd made a breakthrough early in 1971, at the Victorian Championships in Melbourne, when I beat her for the first time, 7–6, 7–6. After six straight losses I'd finally beaten Mighty Maggie, and that's very important to the confidence of both players when it happens after a long stretch of dominance by one of them. The loser knows she doesn't have a pigeon any more. The days of total ownership are over. The winner realizes it can be done, and her confidence surges.

Rod Laver had several tough matches with Stan Smith in 1968 and 1969 and won them. At the end of the year, after Laver had made his Grand Slam and won all he was interested in, they met in an insignificant tournament at Las Vegas. Laver couldn't get his adrenaline going, and Smith won. "A loss for me here, and at this stage of the season, doesn't really matter," Rod said, "except for one thing: Smith now has it in his head that he can beat me. It doesn't matter that I was tired or the conditions were bad, he's beaten Rod Laver for the first time, and he's convinced now that it's possible and should happen again. He's going to be doubly tough for me now."

I don't know if Stan felt the same awe for Laver that I did for Margaret Court, but once you beat somebody they become a little more human and vulnerable to you.

Maybe Margaret, who'd won three Wimbledons, was thinking she had a lot to lose and not much to gain. She was going to be

53

nervous, not transfixed and entranced as she became against Riggs, but the pressure was on her; the people were with me, a big majority of the 14,000 in Centre Court.

I'm glad it didn't rain on my fans who camped that night around the All England Club. They were in good spirits when I arrived Friday, smiling and waving as our limousine pulled through the Doherty Gate. I waved back, feeling like a princess.

When you play Wimbledon, you are picked up by a chauffeur-driven car. But Wimbledon has economized, and players are no longer carried by Rolls Royces and Bentleys. In the old days every player was delivered in the style of an Aga Khan. The prompt, efficient delivery service continues, but the drivers are pretty young women and the cars are a good deal smaller and less ostentatious. The club has made a deal with an auto manufacturer.

But it was a Rolls for us—Mr. and Mrs. Edwards and me—the day of that final, and don't think we didn't love it.

I made the tea that morning and had a cup with Mr. and Mrs. Edwards before breakfast. I could see they were nervous, and it would get worse for them. It's harder to watch somebody you know than to play yourself.

"You're a little better with the tea, these days, Evonne," Mrs. Edwards smiled. I love having her around, and I was glad when Mr. Edwards had phoned her from Paris, after I won the French Open, and asked her to fly from Sydney to London. Mrs. Edwards is like a sister as well as a mother to me. We do a lot of things together. I don't generally take any sweets, and Mrs. Edwards shouldn't—Frank Rostron of the *Daily Express* described her as "an ample mother hen"—but we'll sneak off to a department store called Grace Brothers not far from our home in Roseville to drink iced coffee with whipped cream and ice cream in it. We'll have one, and then Mrs. Edwards will say, "We might have another, Evonne. I won't tell Mr. Edwards if you won't." We spend a lot of time covering up for each other, but Mr. Edwards always knows what's going on anyway.

"Yes, Evonne, you've learned about tea, I reckon," Mrs. Edwards was laughing. That's one of our private jokes. When I first went to live with the Edwardses, and they took me and Trisha around to kids' tournaments, we frequently stayed at motels. That was our treat if we did well. We'd stay at somebody's home for the first couple days of a tournament, but if we played well, Mr. Edwards would splurge on a motel. Motel rooms in Australia are equipped with kettles, teabags, and instant coffee, and the first time we stayed in one Mrs. Edwards asked me to fix the tea.

Some time went by and I hadn't appeared with the tea. "Evonne," Mrs. Edwards called, "what's taking you so long?"

"Well, gee," I answered, "I'm having a lot of trouble getting the tea out of these little bags."

"What?"

"Somebody put the tea in tiny bags, Mrs. Edwards. I don't know if I'm supposed to tear them or what . . ."

Mrs. Edwards and Trisha began laughing so hard they were crying. "Those are teabags, silly," Trisha giggled. "You just drop them in hot water. Didn't you ever see a teabag before?"

The best tea, as any tea drinker will tell you, comes from boiling the leaves in the pot, as we do at home, either at my Mum's or at the Edwardses'. But nobody can accuse me of not being able to handle a teabag any more.

This hurried trip to Wimbledon in 1971 was Mrs. Edwards's first visit to London. She was glad she'd come, pleased I was in the final, and worried I wouldn't play well now that I was one match away from the championship. I was sure I was going to play well—maybe not win, but play well and enjoy myself. I can always tell when I wake up if I'm going to be right and play well. On those days, I usually win. Mrs. Edwards knows that and she'll say, "Well I wish you'd let us know, Evonne. It would save us a lot of worrying and fretting through a match."

I want to run all day. That's the feeling I have when I know I'm going to be right. Some days I get up and I don't have that feeling, and I know it's not my day. I guess I'm fatalistic about it, although sometimes I win anyway. It isn't always up to me, after all. My opponent might be mediocre or have an off day.

I wouldn't want to sit and watch a match with the Edwardses. Mrs. Edwards is all elbows—very sharp elbows. During a match, she'll groan, piercing her companion. Mr. Edwards will fidget and smoke about two packs of cigarettes, going out to pace or grab a beer if he can't stand sitting in one spot. I'd rather play. Of course I get nervous, but I think that just drives me to play better. I'm free to move and run. I'm not confined to a stadium seat. That's like being in the electric chair if you're watching somebody you care about.

Mrs. Edwards had come so far to see her first Wimbledon that she couldn't bear for anything to go wrong. Mr. Edwards said to take it easy. I wasn't supposed to win, and it had been great just to see me get this far. But he had a feeling.

That's what he'd told her over the phone from Paris. The phone rang in Sydney. It was about two in the morning of the next day.

"Are you drunk, Vic?" Mrs. Edwards had been jolted from a sound sleep.

"Just called to wish you a happy anniversary—it's our thirty-fifth, you know."

"Vic, you must be drunk. You never rang me on an anniversary before—"

"And . . . oh yes, Evonne's just won the French. I want you to get the first plane you can for London . . . I've got a feeling about Wimbledon, Eva."

"I've got a feeling you've been drinking, Vic, but it's nice of you to call. I'll catch a plane, too, and you'd better not tell me you don't remember this call when I get to London."

He remembered.

"That's a long, tough way to fly straight through just because you've got a feeling," she told him. "But any time you think Evonne's gonna win Wimbledon I'll swim."

The Rolls called for us, and we were off to Wimbledon. It seemed as good a day as any to drive to the top of my world.

We walked onto Centre Court at two—precisely. Wimbledon is scrupulously punctual; it may be the only tennis tournament in the world that starts on time.

My opponent wasn't all smiles as she had been when we first met in her hometown, Albury, years before. Not ungracious by any means, but I could tell she was a bit tense. She had every reason to be. Although she'd won three Wimbledons and was an old hand playing her tenth, attacks of "Wimbledon nerves" had nipped at her, causing her to fall prior to the final on several previous occasions when she was seeded No. 1 or No. 2.

She had been No. 1 in 1962, and it was too much for her. She lost in the opening round to newcomer Billie Jean King, an unprecedented failure. Never had the first seed lost in the first round. Now she was No. 1 again, and there was no Billie Jean to worry about. I'd beaten her in the semis. Nevertheless, Margaret could sense that Centre Court's adoration of the past had dried up on this afternoon. The greatest of her successes had been achieved on this plot. By the time she accompanied me and the referee, Captain Mike Gibson, into the arena, Margaret Court had won fifty-six of the Big Four (Australian, French, U.S., and Wimbledon) titles in singles, doubles, and mixed doubles. As I write, early in 1974, that total has increased to sixty-three. No man or woman in ninety-seven years of tournament tennis has come close to that figure, and I doubt that anyone ever will. In the matter of winning national championships, Margaret Smith Court is the greatest figure in the history of the game. Possibly she's the best woman ever to play. I've heard about Suzanne Lenglen and Helen Wills and all the Wimbledons they won, but were there as many good players around then? Could they have dealt with Margaret's arms and legs? Those limbs cover so much territory that the court on her side of the net seems to shrink to a green throw rug.

Centre Court can be a cruel place. The devotees won't boo or hiss to show disapproval, although in 1969 Pancho Gonzalez was hooted from the court after protesting referee Gibson's instruction to "play on" in the dusk. Pancho went through the motions, kicking away the second set to Charlie Pasarell before the referee said it was now too dark to play. But Pancho returned the next day, two sets down, and proceeded to win the next three sets, saving seven match points during an extravaganza that ran to a Wimbledon record of 112 games. He departed in a hail of cheers.

Billie Jean, who won in 1966 and 1967 as a bouncy, vivacious young woman, and again in 1968, despite illness, found they didn't love her any more in 1969. An Englishwoman, Ann Jones, was in the final against Billie Jean, and the English seldom have a chance to back one of their own in a Wimbledon title match. Not only was the crowd uncharacteristically boisterous in their support of Mrs. Jones, but they were openly anti-King. In 1972 and 1973, when Billie Jean won again, first over me, and then over Chris Evert, the crowds were all for Chris and me. Billie Jean had won too often for their taste. "I'm the Old Lady now," she said. "They want somebody else to win. But I can take the pressure they put on me."

Now, when Margaret and I went on, there was no question of their expressing disapproval of Margaret. She's been too highly regarded and ladylike for that. She's never drawn the hostility that has befallen Billie Jean, who is an outspoken antiestablishment figure—a "tough broad," as the Americans say. Nevertheless, I think Margaret could feel the overwhelming desire of the crowd for me to beat her. And I didn't help. I played freely and easily, feeling I couldn't miss. For the first time in her long career she could feel a distinct chill in Centre Court: she'd been deserted in favor of a teen-ager. It happens to all champions.

Margaret has been very kind to me—practiced with me, helped me in every way. She has often pointed to me as her successor—although she's taking an awfully long time to leave.

As the Royal Military Academy band played "Waltzing Matilda," a salute to Wimbledon's first all-Australian women's final, the three of us strode onto Centre. The court was faded yet fast: brown and worn down the middle, green on the edges, the grass haggard from two weeks of play, but firm and smooth. The groundsman, Bob Twynam, is an artist. "Courts are to be played on by professionals here, not to be looked at," says Twynam. Twynam, a small, limber, neatly dressed man who has been at Wimbledon a half-century, would roll over gravely ill if he could see them spray-painting the courts green at Forest Hills for the benefit of television.

American grass is impossible; Wimbledon grass is impeccable even though browned. Obviously, they can't raise first-class grass at Forest Hills. It isn't the fault of the groundsman, Ownie Sheridan. Conditions at Forest Hills—heat, humidity, pollution—are against him. Why they don't get rid of it is an agonizing mystery to the players. I expect there'll be a players' strike on the matter one day if the West Side Tennis Club and the U.S. Lawn Tennis Association refuse to provide a decent surface for the U.S. Open, like clay. Until that happens, the spectators as well as the players are being cheated —paying high prices for an inferior product. After all, bad bounces irritate players and spectators alike.

At Wimbledon, however, a bad bounce on Centre Court is an occasion for a parliamentary inquiry. A few of them might mean a change of government. At Forest Hills, once in a while you get a good bounce.

As Margaret, Captain Gibson, and I neared the umpire's chair, we turned to face the Royal Box. Captain Gibson is perfect for the part. Immaculately groomed and barbered in dark suit and mustache, he looks like the retired British army officer that he is. As referee, he is in charge of the operation of the tournament: scheduling of hundreds of players in hundreds of matches on sixteen courts; interpretation of rules in case of a dispute; postponement and resumption of matches interrupted by rain or darkness. The referee's judgment is critical to a tournament, especially one as large and important as Wimbledon. His mistakes don't go unnoticed because London is graced by a tennis press second to none, critics who are literate and perceptive, although at times overly sensational. These writers have millions of readers across Britain, and their impact is tremendous.

The Royal Box, canopied and bordered in blue and gold, is at the south end of the stadium, a twelve-sided enclosure. This stadium, called Centre Court, brings to mind an Elizabethan theater, an open-air playing area surrounded by galleries. There was nothing Shakespearean about what Margaret and I were going to do, but for me it was a midsummer night's dream—and for her a nightmare.

For a moment we faced the Royal Box respectfully, not as subjects of the Queen, beholden to her, but because it's part of the tradition without which Wimbledon would not be Wimbledon. Margaret and I curtsied, as is customary for women, and Captain Gibson bowed. Everybody does this when they come on Centre. Players joke about it. Those from the communist countries are uncomfortable at first because anything royal is anathema to them. Americans think somebody's kidding them when they arrive and learn the protocol. Nevertheless, everybody does it, although awkwardly for the most part. These may be some of the most gifted athletes in the world, but curtsying and bowing don't come naturally to them. Rod Laver says he practically fell on his face the first time.

It's a brief, serious moment, too. You aren't paying homage to royal figureheads; rather, you realize this place is as high as you can go in the career you've chosen, and you are being respectful to all those who helped make it possible—to yourself and to those gathered to watch you.

There isn't much royal about the Royal Box anyway. The occasional princess, duchess, duke, or baron shows up now and again, as do assorted dignitaries and British politicians. For the most part it's filled by tennis officials from all over the world. For these men who make up the International Lawn Tennis Federation—no women are yet represented in the ILTF in this day and age—the Royal Box may be the worst thing that can happen to them. Royal Box Syndrome is all too familiar to tennis players. Once an official has sat there, he's likely to suffer a personality change and believe that he's helping to rule tennis by divine right.

ILTF officials, generally old, wealthy amateurs who are possibly a little more progressive than the reactionary International Olympic Committee, have held the game back way too long. But their control began to erode when open tennis was forced on them in 1968. It will continue to diminish as the players unions (Association of Tennis Pros and Women's Tennis Association) strengthen and the players increasingly chart their own destinies.

The Queen never comes to Wimbledon. She is, in the words of one American sportswriter, a "horse race degenerate"—a horseplayer. Her father, King George VI, was an avid tennis player, and his mother, Queen Mary, a regular in the Royal Box. King George's love for tennis diminished in 1926 though, when he was the young Duke of York. A left-hander, George wasn't exactly a forerunner of Rod Laver, but he was "useful," as the English say. With Sir Louis Grieg, he entered the Wimbledon doubles. It looks, from this distance, as though the draw might have been, shall we say, fiddled a bit. George Windsor and Louis Grieg came up against a pair of ancients in the first round, Arthur Gore, fifty-eight, and Herbert Roper Barrett, fifty-three (who had represented Britain in the first Davis Cup in 1900). Apparently His Royal Highness the Duke of York, as he's listed in the summary, had a bad day on Court Three. With all due respect and deference, the old boys Gore and Barrett won, 6–1, 6–3, 6–2, and the shy, kindly George was so embarrassed he seldom reappeared at Wimbledon.

His mother, Queen Mary, continued her vigil from the Royal Box, although she too suffered a slap in 1926 when she was stood up by the queen of tennis, Suzanne Lenglen. Suzanne, who never lost a singles match at Wimbledon while winning six titles, was scheduled for only a doubles match on the fateful day that caused such a stir across Britain. It's hard to imagine such a hassle today over a tennis player being late for a match, but at Wimbledon, everything is magnified, and tennis can be front-page news during the fortnight of the matches.

When the tournament referee, F. R. Burrow, learned that Queen Mary was coming to Wimbledon that day specifically to watch Suzanne, he changed the schedule and led off his program with Suzanne in a singles at 2:00 P.M. on Centre Court. He neglected, unfortunately, to tell Lenglen. Following normal procedure, a player checks in with the referee before leaving to find out what's on the next day. Suzanne didn't do this. She never had. An official of the club always sought her out to inform her—such was her status. Nobody since has had such a regal position in the game. Nobody, however, contacted Suzanne. It was a slip-up, and she didn't show at the scheduled hour.

Queen Suzanne kept Queen Mary waiting a half-hour, whether by design or through ignorance of the schedule change no one knows. Another match was put on Centre, and eventually Suzanne showed up for her doubles, arriving in the midst of Wimbledon's greatest storm. You can't be beheaded for insulting the Queen any more, but a lot of people thought the block was too good for Suzanne. Others sympathized, and she was rescheduled for another day. Despite public sentiment, which suddenly turned against the darling of Wimbledon, you still couldn't default Queen Suzanne. But the fuss had been too much. She refused to play, and was never seen at Wimbledon again. Later in the year she signed a contract to become the first playing professional, joining a troupe formed by American promoter C. C. (Cash-and-Carry) Pyle.

At my first Wimbledon, 1970, I was actually late for my opening match. No fuss or furor à la Lenglen, happily. I was second match on Court Four, against a French girl, Odile de Roubin, and I was sitting around the dressing room, waiting to play and not paying attention. The players who'd been on the court previously came in, and I should have known it was time for me to go. But I didn't. Nobody told me, and I was a little hazy my first day there.

Presently I got a message from Mr. Edwards: "Hurry, you're on." I was five minutes late, but they overlooked it. I've never let anything like that happen again. At least I wasn't keeping a queen fidgeting in the Royal Box, only Mlle. de Roubin on an outside court. That was bad enough. I apologized, then beat her, 6–1, 6–2.

We laid down our rackets and pocketbooks; the photographers crowded around. Margaret spun a racket to see which of us would serve first. She won the spin and said she'd serve. Now that we were ready for the knock-up—a British expression for warm-up—we were left alone. Alone with the umpire, net judge, foot-fault judge, and ten linesmen and lineswomen. Alone, except for the 14,000 devotees surrounding us and millions freeloading on television. Jammed into the standing-room section, on either side of the court, was the population of Barellan about sixfold—3,000 people who'd bivouacked outside all night. All the seats had been sold out for six months.

I looked around for Mr. and Mrs. Edwards. I was well over my Centre stage fright of the year before. Mr. Edwards was smoking; Mrs. Edwards was knitting. Barry Court, Margaret's husband, was smoking, too, sitting in the row in front of them in a box reserved for friends of the players involved on Centre.

A few practice serves and we were ready to go. I felt very good, like running for the rest of the day. My backhands were shooting along nicely in the warm-up—with either topspin or slice. The umpire said Mrs. Court would serve first, and we were off. There were none of the lavish introductions you get in the United States, telling who we were and what we'd done. At Wimbledon it's taken for granted that everybody knows.

Margaret won three of the first four points, moving to 40–15. I heard groans as I hit a ball into the net. This was a Goolagong crowd. Then Margaret netted one. They weren't going to applaud her mistakes. They wouldn't be rude about it, but you could tell they were glad when Margaret blew one.

Another error, 40–30. And another. Deuce. Margaret was having trouble with her serve. The first ball wasn't going in, and I was swinging away at the second. A sharp backhand, and I had a break point. She served to my backhand, and I rapped it back at her as she closed to make the volley. Margaret couldn't control my return, and I had the first game on a run of four points.

That was a good start.

Where the Goolagongs started out nobody knows. My branch of the family comes from Condobolin, about 125 miles north of Barellan. Roughly halfway between is a town called Goolagong or Gooloogong, depending on how the mapmakers decide to spell it. The residents themselves can't seem to make up their minds. But we Goolagongs aren't from there.

Goolagong is an Aboriginal word meaning tall trees by still water. Teddy Tinling, the tennis dressmaker, designed a dress for me with trees and a stream flowing by at the hemline. Chris Evert was curious: "What is that—an oasis in the Sahara Desert?"

"Just my name," I said. "In living color."

We used to go back to Condobolin a lot when I was young to see my father's family. There were a large Aboriginal settlement and a lot of kids to play with. These were the only times I've spent with my people, and they were great times. People would sit around fires at night, the way Aborigines did when the country was ours, and there'd be dancing—a corroboree—to the music of the didjeridu, a wooden pipe made from a tree trunk. Aborigines tend to stick together if they can. My father, Ken Goolagong, did all right as a shearer in Barellan, but I don't think he ever felt that he fit into the white community. We went back to Condobolin as often as we could.

Dad felt that whites looked down on him. He couldn't escape this feeling, and he'd be very morose about it sometimes, but you couldn't get him to talk about it. My father is a very quiet, withdrawn man, while my mother is cheery and outgoing. I've never been able to find out what experiences in Dad's past put him on the defensive, and I've never known him to be discriminated against. I do know that he's liked in Barellan; he plays at the local golf club and drinks at the War Memorial Club just like everyone else.

"Ken'll shear his 200," you'll hear the men say. That means that with the electric clippers he can defrock 200 sheep a day, which is going some and makes a shearer respected. He'll never wipe out the memory of the legendary Jackie Howe, who did 320 ewes in 8 hours and 20 minutes. And he did it with hand clippers! (Shaking hands with Jackie Howe must have been an excruciating experience.) But my Dad is a good man at his trade. The trouble is, it's an irregular and a very hard business. It takes a very supple man with a very strong back. A shearer, if he's lean like Dad, is limber enough to stand on a curb and bend over and touch the street with the flat of his hands, without bending his knees.

From what I know of my background, my bloodline is quite good for an athlete—I come from hardy people. My grandfather on my mother's side, Eric Briggs, was also a shearer, moving around where the work was as my Dad does now. Roy Goolagong, my father's father, worked on the railroad in the west out of Broken Hill, "driving the dogs" (spikes), as they say. He was so well thought of that he was permitted to go to the hotel and drink with the men back in 1946, at a time when most saloons were off-limits to Aborigines.

It didn't hurt my becoming a strong server to have all those rugged backbones in my family tree. Serving is easier than laying ties or shearing sheep any day. I don't know much about railroad work, but I've seen the long, physically exhausting days Dad puts in—dragging, lifting, and maneuvering those big, reluctant sheep inside a sweltering shed, amidst the overpowering din of the engine that keeps the clippers going.

There was never any doubt in Dad's mind that I should leave that country when I had the opportunity, for his life has been day after day of counting sheep the hard way: grinding monotony.

I don't think he and Mum could quite understand that playing a game could be a way of advancing myself, of supporting myself, eventually, and of traveling the world. But Dad, especially, thought it was worth a try. Mum agreed with him, although she says now, "I was scared I'd never see Evonne again. I worried all the time about her going off alone, that she'd get sick. I missed her something awful, but after she'd been with the Edwardses I knew they was taking good care of her."

I'd write home, and Dad or one of the kids would read my letters to Mum. She can't read or write. She dropped out of school almost as soon as she started. In 1970, the first year I traveled overseas with Mr. Edwards and Trisha Edwards as my doubles partner, we were discussing sending cassette tapes back home instead of letters. It would be easier just talking to people.

"That'll be perfect for your Mum," said Mr. Edwards.

"But," I said, "she's never had a tape machine. Suppose she can't figure out how to work it—"

Mr. Edwards replied, "That's easy. She just has to read the instructions. They're very simple . . ."

We looked at each other, then broke up, while Trish was saying, "But Mrs. Goolagong can't read, Dad, that's the whole idea." Mum laughed, too, when I told her.

In Italy they call me Chocolata, which amuses me. I guess I'd call me honey-colored. Mum and Dad aren't sure how much Aborigine blood is in us, but to my mind I'm an Australian first. I realize this has brought some criticism on me by some Aborigines who feel I should be more political about the Aborigine struggle and spend more time with my people. I am anxious to learn more about them, but right now tennis keeps me away from Australia. Besides, I'm a nonpolitical person, and I'm not ashamed of that.

The press, obviously, has hammered away at my origins: it's a good story. I'm the first Aborigine in tennis and one of a few to win a world championship in any sport. At first, though, when I was coming up, I was very embarrassed by the publicity because I knew I was getting it on the basis of color, not ability. I was a freak. I wasn't playing well enough to warrant all the attention I got when I moved to Sydney for good. It bothered me all the more because I was trying to settle into Willoughby High School and be just like everybody else. But there was all the publicity, and what I wanted most was to improve so much that if the publicity continued, I would at least be worth it as a tennis player.

After a while I thought the references to me as an Aborigine were overdone, and they still are in some places. When the publicity began noticeably in 1964, this was a typical headline:

SELECTORS PRAISE COLOURED 12-YEAR-OLD

That was from the Wagga Wagga *Daily Advertiser*. I was big in Wagga Wagga.

Or:

BRILLIANT YOUNG ABORIGINAL
TENNIS STAR YVONNE GOOLAGONG
MAKES 1ST WAGGA APPEARANCE

It was always colored this or Aboriginal that—and for years they misspelled my name as Yvonne. My mother named me Evonne Fay because, as she said, "I didn't know anybody with those names. I wanted her to have different, special names. And I purposely spelled it E-V-O-N-N-E so it would be her own, different from all the Yvonnes with Y's." Mum knew enough about spelling to do that. It was years before we could convince the journalists.

Anybody could see I was Aboriginal. I'm honored to have made the Aboriginal breakthrough in tennis, and I hope many more follow, but there comes a time when that constant racial identification should be dropped, as Arthur Ashe, the American black, requested a few years ago. He was always being referred to as a Negro tennis star, and finally, in 1965, when he made his Davis Cup debut, Arthur said to reporters, "I appreciate all you've written, but you don't keep referring to Willie Mays as a Negro in your stories, do you? We know he's black, but all people care about now is how he plays. I think that's all people should care about in my case."

I'll concede it was newsworthy in my case when in 1971 I was granted a South African visa and became the first nonwhite to play against whites in a tennis tournament in that country. It became important again in 1973, when, after being twice refused, Ashe did get a South African visa. Then race had to figure in the stories because both Arthur and I had broken color barriers (along with several other nonwhite players in the South African Opens of 1971, 1972, and 1973).

I lost the South African final, as defending champion, in 1973 to Chris Evert, 6–3, 6–3, after having scads of break points throughout the second set.

"Sad, sad," said Mrs. Edwards when I came off the court, trying to be of some consolation.

Sad? Had somebody died? Then I realized she meant the match. Oh, that? It was over, past. "Nothing to be sad about," I said.

What's past is past. After I broke Margaret in the opening game at Wimbledon, of course I served and we went right to a break point for her at 30–40. It looked as though my quick start would be canceled out. But I hit a pretty good serve and came in behind it to make a volley. Deuce. I guess I smiled. Fourteen thousand people around me seemed to be smiling in relief. Didn't anybody want Margaret to win? Certainly. Barry Court was with her all the fretting, fuming way, sitting there just in front of the Edwardses, he and Mr. Edwards in their own competition to see who could smoke the most.

Larry King, Billie Jean's husband, went on a bonbon trip his first time at Wimbledon in 1966, watching her win her first singles title. "I had to have something to do with my hands," says Larry, "and I became a candy junkie, going through bags of those wonderful bonbons they sell at Wimbledon. Terrible for my teeth, but better than smoking. If things were going really bad in one of Billie Jean's matches I'd cop out by reading a book. But that's cowardly, I know."

I won the next two points, and had a 2–0 lead. Not bad. Nobody had gotten more than two games off Margaret in the tournament except another Australian, Judy Tegart Dalton, in the semis, who won the first set. Then Margaret finished Judy off, 4–6, 6–1, 6–0. A 0–2 deficit was nothing serious for Margaret. Still, it was her poorest start of the fortnight.

On a May morning in 1962 my parents put me on the Sydney plane at Narrandera. I had seen planes far off in the sky. Now I was on one, flying higher than a galah, headed for Sydney, a place I'd always wanted to see.

But did I want to, now that I was on the plane? I'd seen pictures of Sydney, but I couldn't really picture it. Towns of five or six thousand people were huge to me. Sydney had more than a million.

Would these people, the Edwardses, like me? Would I like them? Would I know how to act? Would I be able to hit a ball properly, or did the kids in Sydney hit too hard and fast for a bushie? Suppose they didn't like me . . . or I couldn't play very well? Would they scold me and send me home right away?

There wasn't a lot of time to think about all this, but I was nervous. I was balling a handkerchief in my hand and wondering how this airplane could settle itself safely on the ground, although I knew it would.

On the loudspeaker the pilot was saying we were landing, and down there was Sydney . . . unbelievable . . . so many houses, a red sea of tile roofs . . . but then—the real sea, the harbor . . . gorgeous glittering blue with all those boats—all so new and stunning. Buildings rose everywhere, much taller than Barellan's wheat silos. Out beyond the harbor was the ocean, my first glimpse of water broader than the Murrumbidgee River.

"It's too big. Sydney's too big for me," was my first thought. I wondered if I'd cry, but I was also telling myself: "You see it out. It's only for a couple of weeks, and then you'll be back home."

Jean Gladman had taken an interest in me. She was the wife of a grazier my father worked for. She got me a suitcase and helped me pack. She bought me some clothes and dressed me for the trip. "I'll never forget how Evonne looked that day," Trisha always says. She closes her eyes. "Evonne had on a red coat, a plaid skirt, and a little white hat. A funny little white hat," Trisha smiles.

Mrs. Gladman loaned me one of my first rackets, and this racket was the cause of what I remember as the greatest explosion of my life. My baby sister, Janelle (who has the ability to play on the international circuit, if she'll apply herself), was playing on the floor. Nobody was paying much attention to her when she came across the racket and started to examine it. Suddenly she pitched it into the wood fire in the fireplace. It was gone, just like that.

I was enraged. I really blew up at her, screamed at her, cried, wanted to pound her, but I didn't. I was furious at first, then worried and mournful, practically bereaved. Not only was my most valued possession gone—but it wasn't even mine. What would Mrs. Gladman

69

say about my carelessness with her racket? Where would I get another? How was I going to play again?

Dad wasn't very happy either because Mr. Gladman deducted the cost of the racket from his pay. But once that was done, and I was cautioned to watch over my belongings more carefully, Mrs. Gladman loaned me another racket.

When I got off the plane I had a new racket that Mr. Kurtzman had given me, and the Edwardses spotted me right away. Mrs. Edwards, Trisha, and Jenifer were smiling and waving. They'd driven to the airport with Mr. Edwards.

"We go over the bridge to the northern suburbs, to Roseville," said Mrs. Edwards. Once more we were high above the harbor on the bridge. They stopped to hand a man some money. Mrs. Edwards knew there'd be a lot of explaining to do. "We pay every time we go across," she said. "This is a toll bridge."

"We have a bridge over the river at home," I said, "but you don't have to pay to get across." Things were very strange in this city.

Eva Prentice Edwards comes from Angledool up on the New South Wales–Queensland border, near the opal mines at Lightning Ridge. She's a country girl herself, and I think that's why she's always understood me so well. She was also a very good tennis player, school-girl champion of New South Wales. She was good enough in those days to beat Joan Hartigan, who would go on to win the Australian women's title three times during the 1930s. Mrs. Edwards's father, who owned a large cattle property, sent her to convent school in Sydney, and she became one of the elder Mr. Edwards's tennis pupils. That's how she met Vic. Her knowledge of the country, of Aborigines —many of whom worked for her father—and of tennis made me feel right at home with her. Mrs. Edwards is a friend and mother. Only her daughters Jenifer and Trisha are closer to me. I think I play my best when she's traveling with me. She understands I have to get out and away from tennis. We go sightseeing, something I never do when I travel with Mr. Edwards. We collect china and paint on china as well. Her interests are broader than Mr. Edwards's. He kids us, "How were things in the secondhand shops?" when we've been looking at antiques. Or says, "No thanks, I don't want to see another rockpile," when we ask him if he wants to go sightseeing at a ruin or cathedral.

The Edwardses have a big comfortable house they built on War-rane Street after World War II, just around the corner from the Victor A. Edwards Tennis School. It's handsomely landscaped with roses, bougainvillaea, jacaranda, and a variety of other flowers. In back there's a loam tennis court. "There's my business," Mr. Edwards says, pointing in the direction of VAETS, "but here's my interest"—the backyard court.

On that court he can work privately with the pupils to whom he pays closest attention. Fred Stolle, one of the great Australians who won the U.S. singles at Forest Hills in 1966, used to drill with Mr. Edwards in the backyard early in the morning before going to work at a Sydney bank and then drilled again in the evening. Bob Hewitt, Jan Lehane O'Neill, and many others have done the same. When I'm home that's where I practice. It's quiet, there's nobody around, and we can get a lot done. There's no escaping a tennis court when you live with Victor Edwards. Lucky for me I didn't want to escape.

The first time I was in Sydney only for two weeks, but I was terribly homesick. I didn't know if I could make myself come back to Sydney again, if I was invited, but I knew I had to. The plan was for me to spend the three school holidays a year at the Edwardses. Two weeks at Easter, two weeks at the end of May, and the longest—eight weeks—over Christmas and the New Year, although I wouldn't spend the entire eight weeks. I'd be with my own family for Christmas.

Trisha, a year younger than me and a promising player, said, when we met, "You'll be living with me, in my room. I hope you like it." It was the nicest room I'd ever seen, although there's nothing fancy about the Edwards place. A nice, comfortable stone house. That in itself was an oddity. All the houses in Barellan are what they call fibros, fiberboard with metal roofs of corrugated tin. Our house, the old newspaper building, was all metal. Extra cold in the winter, extra hot in the summer.

I liked Trisha's room so much that I never moved out, although I'm not there much either. But it's my room now. Trisha's married

71

and living on the other side of Sydney, in Manly. Jenifer's gone, living with a group of young wanderers on a double-decker bus they've made into a mobile home. I'm the last of the Edwards girls left in the house.

Every tennis coach plots, schemes, and dreams about having a Wimbledon champion, but I don't think a coach ever raised one in his own family until I won for Mr. Edwards. (Jimmy Evert, Chris's father, was the next.) In the third game against Margaret, with me ahead 2–0, Mr. Edwards must have sensed that this might indeed be the day—though, by his calculations, I was three years premature.

Margaret was serving for the second time, and it was becoming a long game. We were both pretty cautious, rallying from the baseline, which wasn't like us, waiting for mistakes. She seemed to feel that I was bound to come apart a little after my quick start, and I couldn't quite believe that I'd won the first two games. I'd get a break point and then make a mistake, and we'd be at deuce—three times at deuce. She was straining hard to get into the match now, and I was starting to feel looser, freer, and stronger with every point. I was enjoying myself. It was glorious running on the grass. Like dancing, fast dancing. Everything seems faster on a grass court because the ball stays low, skids, spurts at you instead of bounding lazily the way it does on a clay court. Serves hit the court and dart this way and that. Your reflexes have to be sharper and quicker to cope. There's less time to make the stroke; you're lunging, leaping, sprinting instead of loping. It's like being part of a speeded-up movie, and that's my style: fast. That's why I like grass so much.

Another break point, the fourth. Then Margaret hit a ball wide and I had another game, 3–0. We changed ends of the court. She took her time, trying to pull herself together. She looked at me, as though to say, "I'll catch you, don't you worry." But she said nothing. Margaret knew she had to summon all the concentration and determination that had made her the most successful and feared player in the women's game. It hadn't been easy for Margaret Smith Court. She was no natural. She worked for her championships, drove herself through a training regimen that would make most male athletes faint. She ran, did calisthenics, weight training, and practiced . . . practiced . . . practiced . . .

Her goal was, basically, to be right here on Centre Court, Wimbledon. The rest is fine, splendidly remunerative, and there is better prize money elsewhere, but Wimbledon is what we all want above everything else. I don't know if every Catholic priest would like to become pope. But every tennis player wants to win The Lawn Tennis Championships, and Wimbledon is our Vatican.

I would be serving at 3–0. I shook my head as I walked to the baseline, unable to quite accept that Margaret hadn't yet won a game. I was two breaks up after three games. Then I know I smiled because the applause was coming down from all sides, sounding like big surf at Bondi Beach.

Play and practice. Practice and play. I'm not an authority on other sports, but I can't see how any athlete would practice and play more than a tennis player.

Everywhere in the world someone is practicing tennis every hour of the day. I don't worry about it. To me it means only that somebody will always be popping up to have a go at beating me. Somebody I've never heard of is whacking balls against a wall right now—just as I was doing the day Margaret Court won her first Wimbledon in 1963 —and getting ready for me.

I went back to Barellan, and I was glad to return to the country. Two weeks in Sydney had been quite enough for starters. I liked the Edwardses, but their city frightened me. It was too big and fast. I missed the bush where time seems endless. There's time for everything.

Mr. Edwards, on a trip in the country, once stopped for gas in a place that wasn't much more than a gas station, the indispensable hotel, and a few houses. The man who ran the station was changing a tire when a shout came from the hotel bar across the road: "Hey, Will, your old man just dropped dead!"

"Hang on until I get this tire done, mate," said Will.

You don't rush country people. In Sydney the rush never seemed to end.

That didn't mean I was casual and slow about tennis when I got back to Barellan. I'd learned a few things about stroking from Mr. Edwards, and I knew I had a lot of improving to do. In Barellan we kids would go to the courts early in the morning and play after supper under the lights till ten or eleven o'clock. Sometimes there'd be frost on the ground for those early and late sessions in the winter, and we'd be shivering. Running warmed us up quick enough.

Mr. Kurtzman continued to take me around to the weekend tournaments at places like Ganmain, where one of the cement courts had a big hole in it. You tried to hit the hole—it was an automatic point. The ball just died there. These tournaments kept me busy. I might play six different events over a weekend, the under-eighteen singles and doubles and the adult women's singles and doubles, plus a couple of handicap events.

It got so that when people saw Mr. Kurtzman at a tournament they'd say, "Here's the man who came to carry home all the trophies." This wasn't a very high standard of tennis, but I was on the court, playing constantly. My strokes weren't very good, I knew, but they were coming along. I was winning a lot with my legs. I was also starting an endless process of acquiring things I couldn't use. Trophies. Prizes. The first thing I won was a pen, when I was eight, in a club tournament at Barellan. Then there were comb and brush sets. At Ganmain I won a women's tournament, and first prize was a pair of sheets. I guess they noticed my twelve-year-old face falling when I saw the sheets, so they exchanged them for a cosmetic kit.

Competition is the essence of Australian tennis. No matter who you are or what level you play at, there's a competition for you, a tournament or a team or club competition. We haven't gone as far as the United States where their age-group tournaments extend above seventy-five years of age. When Bobby Riggs wins the seventy-five's, he'll probably challenge Billie Jean King again. She'll be forty-nine.

But in Australia I think we have more varieties of competition than anywhere else. After I moved to Sydney for good in 1965, I was playing plenty of the usual tournaments in my own age group and above. And I was also playing for the Chatswood Club in one league on clay courts and for White City in another on grass courts. Then there were district and state tournaments and teams and national events. It never stopped. You'd be involved in two or three competitions simultaneously.

You needed somebody else to keep up with what you were doing so that all you had to do was check the schedule and be on court at the appointed time. Although tennis pretty much excluded me from other activities, my closest friends were in the game. Other friends at school learned not to invite me anywhere on a weekend because I'd be playing tennis. Whenever I felt I might be missing something, I reminded myself that this was what I had to do to get ahead in tennis. I'd be giving up some things to get what I wanted most.

Mr. Kurtzman's original request—that Mr. Edwards take me into his home—had led to my vacation stays in Sydney. Those were good for my tennis, but they weren't enough. Mr. Edwards was well aware of this. After my thirteenth birthday, he had a "crucial" talk with Mr. Kurtzman.

"Bill," he said," you were absolutely right when you singled Evonne out. I've come to believe that she can go all the way to the top of tennis. But there's only one way this can happen: she has to come live with us full time, be a part of our family. If she does this she becomes my child. I don't mean legally, or that she turns her back on her people. But that I'm in charge of her just as I am of my daughters Trisha and Jenifer and as I was of my other three daughters before they were married. The discipline, education, the living habits, the tennis. Everything.

"This is the only way it can be accomplished. We're all very fond of Evonne. Eva and the girls have taken to her in a big way. They're all for it. She can move in with Trisha. As you know, they've played doubles together when Evonne's visited us, and I think they can become one of the finest teams in the world.

75

"But, Bill, what are you and the people of Barellan prepared to do, even if this is all right with Melinda and Ken Goolagong? Evonne's welcome in my home, but I can't pay for her entire upkeep . . ."

Mr. Kurtzman said he understood. He said that he'd have to talk to my parents and that he'd get together with some of the men at the War Memorial Club to see what could be done to raise money for my support.

Leaving for good? At thirteen? Mum and Dad gave their blessing —not entirely happily, but by this time they realized that tennis was my way of life, and that Sydney was the only place for me to get on. They were glad the Edwardses were taking an interest, and my Dad regretted he couldn't afford to help out. I suppose he's always been a little troubled that he couldn't provide the financial support he would have liked. He shouldn't be. He did his best to provide for eight kids, and he took care of us all right. I was seeking a rather specialized education, and what I got amounted to sort of a scholarship.

It wasn't the first time that townspeople had gotten together in Australia to contribute to a fund so that one of the community's youngsters could get ahead in tennis. They did it in Grenfell to finance Jan Lehane O'Neill's first overseas trip. A wealthy businessman underwrote Rod Laver's first overseas tour when Rod was a teen-ager.

But before I could think of going abroad I had to settle in Sydney. That's what Mr. Kurtzman had to sell when he made his pitch at a meeting at the War Memorial Club.

"We can't let this little girl of ours down," he said to his friends. "This is her chance—our chance, too, to get recognition for Barellan. Vic Edwards is confident she can become a champion. Wouldn't it be wonderful for Barellan to have a champion—for the first Aboriginal champion to have been given the opportunity by us?"

He worked on their civic pride and their heartstrings, and he got results. It's impossible for me ever to repay their warm and generous spirit. The Goolagong fund amounted to $934, spread over three years. It was six dollars a week that Bill Kurtzman sent to Mr. Edwards for my upkeep. This went on for three years until, I guess, they felt I was established.

I don't know how many men were involved. I meet a lot of them who say they were, and I take them at their word. It wouldn't have been much from each one to come to six dollars. And yet, they were giving with no thought to any return. These were men who had done pretty well on wheat and sheep, but they had known hard times, too. They were at the mercy of nature and always had been. People like that don't throw money around. I appreciate the generosity of six dollars a week. Without it, I'd never have gotten to Sydney.

Bill Kurtzman died at the age of seventy-eight during the summer of 1973. His death touched me deeper than anything I'd known. When Mr. Edwards told me, I just wanted to be alone and cry. For several days I was shaken and depressed. Gradually I realized there was nothing I could do. It's not my nature to be sad for long. If I'm down I can snap out of it by playing tennis; I lose myself in the game. I've thought a lot about what this kind old man had done for me and for Barellan. Priscilla Kurtzman, his widow, who continues to live in Barellan, has told me, "Evonne, you were Bill's life."

Clearly $934 didn't cover the care and feeding and transporting of Evonne Goolagong from 1965 until I picked up my first prize money check in 1970. That was just a down payment, and Mr. Edwards paid the rest, like any good father who could afford it. He did this, I should point out, well before there was any hope of open tennis becoming a reality. Prior to 1968, when opens—the integration of amateurs and professionals, with prize money at stake for the pros— were at last approved by the International Lawn Tennis Federation, there was no money in the game for women.

Pro tennis existed, barely, and only for a few men such as Rod Laver, Ken Rosewall, Pancho Gonzalez, Andres Gimeno, and Lew Hoad. An elite clique of so-called amateurs—with Roy Emerson, Manolo Santana, Nicola Pietrangeli, Marty Mulligan, Rafe Osuna in the lead—were doing well on exorbitant "expense" payments. If there was any money left over, Margaret Court, Billie Jean King, Maria Bueno, and Ann Jones picked up a nice share, passed under the mythical table. A career as such was not open to female tennis players. Billie Jean, tired of the under-the-table dealings, said—to her credit

—"I'm a pro, in actuality if not in name. Let's do away with this amateur lie and all be pros and play for prize money."

Phony amateurism had pretty much vanished by the time I went onto the international circuit. I wouldn't have enjoyed bargaining and haggling with tournament promoters for my services. I suppose Mr. Edwards would have handled most of it, but the thought doesn't appeal to me. I don't pay attention to the money anyway. I'm in the game for a life, not a living, and I'd be playing as an amateur if a professional career wasn't possible.

The money is beyond belief today, but Mr. Edwards wasn't thinking about that and neither was I. We both just wanted to see how far up I could go. I'm sure he would have backed me if I hadn't made a shilling. As it turned out I grossed about $250,000 in prize money during my first five years as a professional—$103,600 for 1973—and just about that much in endorsement contracts.

Biggest of all is the contract I signed with the Pittsburgh Triangles in the radical new World Team Tennis League, guaranteeing me $1 million over five years and some other fringe benefits, but permitting me the option to leave if I'm not happy.

Chuck Reichblum, Frank Fuhrer, and Bill Sutton, who operated the Triangles, kept trying to press the $1 million on me, but Mr. Edwards and I didn't make it easy on them.

We said, "No, no, a million times no . . ."

While they were saying, "Can't we at least discuss it?"

And we said, "No, no, a million . . ."

But they kept saying, "Please, let's . . ."

Still, that word "million" kept coming up, and Mr. Edwards and I surprised ourselves by signing contracts to join the Pittsburgh Triangles organization in a league that began its revolutionary operation in May 1974. Mr. Edwards signed a good contract, too, as general manager and adviser to the player-coach, Ken Rosewall.

Would World Team Tennis be successful? That was the question administrators, promoters, tournament organizers, players, journalists, and fans started asking midway through 1973 when sixteen city franchises at $50,000 apiece were made available. All were purchased (a couple resold at a profit immediately), and the owners held a player draft in New York at which their ignorance of tennis was second only to their obliviousness to losing money. Larry King (Billie Jean's husband) and Jordan Kaiser and Dennis Murphy (two of the founders of the young World Hockey Association) were the leaders in getting WTT started, along with Fred Barman (father of player Shari Barman). George MacCall, once a U.S. Davis Cup captain, then head of the National Tennis League (a pro circuit in the early days of open tennis that was absorbed by Lamar Hunt's World Championship Tennis), was hired as commissioner.

Tennis has been essentially a tournament game played by individuals, but team matches—country against country—in Davis, Federation, Wightman, World, Bell, and King's Cups are intensely competitive and very exciting. The idea of city teams playing a full schedule of indoor matches over a definite period (May to August) was novel. Would Detroiters support the Detroit Loves as fervently as they do the Tigers of baseball, the Redwings of hockey, the Pistons of basketball, or the Lions of football? Could Pittsburghers find room in their hearts for the Triangles, hearts already filled with the Pirates, Steelers, and Penguins? Would people turn out to watch the Philadelphia Freedoms led by player-coach Billie Jean King against the Minnesota Buckskins led by player-coach Owen Davidson? Would the Boston Lobsters be baked, stuffed, or boiled despite the presence of Kerry Melville and Roger Taylor?

Compounding the novelty was the blending of men and women together on a pro team for the first time in sport. In the WTT format, an evening's program consisted of five one-set matches—men's and women's singles and doubles plus mixed doubles—with the result based on total number of games won. Statistics and standings were tabulated as in other sports, and the best teams from four divisions entered championship playoffs at the close of the season, an American concept applied to most of their pro games. Substitution was permitted—an incredible innovation for tennis. If you weren't doing well, the coach could pull you out and put somebody else in. Chicago brought in left-hander Ray Ruffels—like a relief pitcher—to serve the last game of the night and preserve a one-game victory over Houston. Tennis had never experienced anything like it, and neither had the game's followers, who either suffered or cheered through what they considered either a corruption or an amusing variation of their game.

Even the scoring was different: VASSS No-ad, in which every game is "sudden death." VASSS (Van Alen Streamlined Scoring System) was devised by the Newport Bolshevik, Jimmy Van Alen, the scoring radical who fathered tie-breakers to eliminate long deuce sets. Under No-ad, no game can last more than seven points, no set more than thirteen games. If the score is three-points-all (deuce in traditional scoring), you are at sudden death (as at four-points-all in his nine-point tie-breaker). The seventh point is the last. Receiver has choice of court. Suddenly it's all over. No deuce-advantage back-and-forth possibilities. This is hard to get used to after growing up in the conventional system. Tie-breakers at six-games-all are a good innovation, but No-ad seems too much. However, the American public may want a fast-paced match involving many faces in two-and-a-half hours' time for an evening's entertainment, and they get it with this system. Moreover, I found myself concentrating better after my initial discomfort in WTT because every single point really *is* important. You can't let up for an instant—every game you lose counts for the other team.

Nobody thought WTT would actually get started, but by springtime the sixteen teams had coaches and full rosters and were in varying states of readiness. The tennis establishment was alarmed. There's a trend, which I don't think anybody likes, of big-money tennis centering more and more in America as professional golf has. WTT signed on many of the best players at fabulous sums. Practically all the top women except Chris Evert signed. Tom Okker, in becoming player-coach of Toronto-Buffalo got a base salary of $136,000 plus a bonus of $200 for every game he won! Only in America.

Since the WTT season covered the summer (with three weeks out for Wimbledon and an acclimatizing week prior to it on grass), tennis promoters and administrators in Europe and America were fearful that their own customary tournament seasons would be drained of name players, diminished in stature and appeal. WTT promised time off for any of its players who wished to enter the Italian or French Opens, in addition to Wimbledon, or join their national teams in Davis and Federation Cup play. I wouldn't have signed without this option.

But the option was negated by a bloc of European nations within the International Lawn Tennis Federation, and I got caught in a ban along with a lot of others who signed up with WTT. Worried about their tournaments and determined to fight WTT, these nations—led by France—made their events off-limits to us. That was a blow, particularly to Jimmy Connors of Baltimore and me. Since we'd won the Australian Open titles early in 1974, Jimmy and I were the only players in the world who could possibly make a Grand Slam. But the next leg was the French Open, and we couldn't win it if we couldn't play it. Both of us flew to Paris for the tournament, feeling the French officials would relent. They didn't, and Mr. Edwards decided we would join with Connors and his agent in suing the French Federation for restraining our freedom in our livelihood. It's in the hands of lawyers as I write, and no one knows when or if it will ever come to trial. No court can give you a title or retrieve a missed opportunity. It was another political hassle that was beyond my interest or grasp, but it hurt because I'd like to be the third woman to make a Grand Slam (Maureen Connolly in 1953 and Margaret Court in 1970 were the other two). Probably it hurt Connors more, as matters turned out, because he eventually won the third and fourth legs—Wimbledon and the U.S. Open. He could claim justifiably that a silly stand by the French cost him a chance at a rare achievement, as well as a lot of money. A manufacturer of male cosmetics offered a $100,000 bonus for any man who could make a Grand Slam. Similarly, I may have missed out on a huge bonus—the $125,000 offered by Chesebrough-Pond's for a Slam, or the $35,000 for the woman who did best in Slam tournaments. Chris Evert, who won the French, barely beat me out for the latter.

Fortunately—and sensibly—Wimbledon and the British LTA

didn't go along with the ILTF members who banned us. Exclusion from Wimbledon would have made me deeply regret signing with Pittsburgh.

Only a Henry Kissinger could unravel tennis politics to the satisfaction and understanding of everybody. I just play and hope for the best. I wasn't enthralled by the prospect of WTT, although it turned out to be a lot of fun and I'm going to try it again in 1975. I didn't even think about WTT when the league's early plans were being made. I noticed that Billie Jean signed with Philadelphia and Margaret Court with the Golden Gaters of the San Francisco Bay Area. But Mr. Edwards was dead against it, and the idea of indoor tennis made me claustrophobic. That's the word all right: indoor tennis gives me claustrophobia. I don't like it. My worst stretch in tennis was the Dewar Circuit in Britain during the autumn of 1971—all indoors. Admittedly the locations and the weather weren't very attractive. I traveled alone, and I got back to Australia sick and rundown. Indoor tourneys in America haven't thrilled me either, although generally the facilities are first-rate.

So why am I a Pittsburgh Triangle? When you realize athletes have only a limited number of years at the top, the kind of money Fuhrer, Reichblum, and Sutton were talking did become attractive. Nevertheless they had an awful hard time forcing $1 million down our bank accounts. Mr. Edwards kept saying, "Go away . . . not interested." This wasn't a bargaining ploy, or the old come-on. We were not in the least curious.

These three men were getting frustrated and thought us a bit rude in not even listening to their proposition. They contacted Bud Stanner, our man at International Management. "Sorry, I know you have a good reputation," said Stanner, "but Vic and Evonne just aren't interested. They don't like the idea, the dates, the conditions, or the possibility of a ban."

Reichblum, Fuhrer, and Sutton decided to fight stubbornness with stubbornness. They flew to Toronto during the Canadian Open, which precedes Forest Hills. They came up to our table during dinner and wouldn't go away until we said, "O.K., we'll listen to what you have to say." The meal was getting cold. We agreed to meet with them and our agents.

I won't go into all the details, benefits, guarantees, whereas's, provisions, escape hatches, and so on. Essentially, Mr. Edwards decided, "Honey, it's worth a try for both of us. It makes you and your family financially secure for life, regardless of whether the league collapses or an injury ends your career. You'll be right forever. It looks once in a lifetime to me and our agents." I had the privilege of withdrawing if and when team tennis no longer satisfied me and canceling out the remainder of the contract. So we signed.

I wondered, would they love me in Pittsburgh as they did in Wagga Wagga? I found Pittsburgh to be a very friendly city. Maybe it was my destiny to go from one town of three rivers to another. Barellan, in Aborigine, means "meeting of the waters." The waters, which seldom exist, are Mirool Creek, Sandy Creek, and Colinroobie Runner. Coming together outside of town, they're usually represented by three dry gulches. Pittsburgh's Golden Triangle is formed by the confluence of the bustling Allegheny, Monongahela, and Ohio rivers.

About 10,000 very noisy people turned up at the Spectrum in Philadelphia for the inauguration of WTT on May 6: Pittsburgh against Billie Jean's Freedoms. I thought I'd walked into a carnival by mistake. Bands were playing, including one called the Mummers String Band dressed in huge fluffy costumes that made them look like a walking jungle. People were cheering. On the balcony facing the courts was a variety of signs of the sort you see at basketball and hockey games, praising the home players and knocking the opponents. One sign said: EVONNE—BE GONE.

Soon I wished I was gone—a long way from WTT. It was so strange and crazy at first. Tennis players are conditioned to silence during the points. In WTT the crowd never shuts up. They're encouraged to yell, and sometimes it's way out of order. I was terribly embarrassed when we played Boston and several fans yelled, "Kerry, you stink!" at Kerry Melville. That wasn't the worst of it. Nobody liked the insulting remarks ("Billie Jean wears after-shave!" "Hey, Tiriac, why don't you go back to the old monsters home?"). But sometimes it was funny. Nobody was immune. You had to get used to screams of "double fault!" and "choke!" when you served.

At first, it was unbearable. I wondered what I'd gotten into. It was time for the pleasant tournaments in Rome and Paris and throughout England, and here I was acting like a performing seal in a circus. I wanted out. Mr. Edwards said, "Let's give it a chance for a while, honey. I think we owe them that." Worse than the noise and the hecklers was the travel. The league stretched from Hawaii to Boston, from Minnesota to Miami, and we might play three nights running in three different cities. I'd be walking around in a daze. We'd finish playing late at night and then catch a plane, or else we'd get up early the next morning and head for the airport. I'd never minded traveling until this crazy schedule of one-nighters. It was hard on everybody. The rhythm of one-set tennis was difficult to adjust to. Somehow I beat Billie Jean 6–2 in that opener, but I lost the next five sets I played. Philadelphia beat us 31–25 in the league's first meeting, and we were off to a slow start.

We tied for first in our division with Detroit and made the playoffs, and I won most of my sets. We beat Detroit in the first round and lost to Philadelphia in the second, but Denver came in strong at the end to take the championship over the Freedoms, 27–21 and 28–24. That pleased us because Denver's player-coach was Tony Roche, another bushie from New South Wales. One of the more satisfying matches was a 28–24 win for us over Philadelphia, which stopped an eighteen-match winning streak of theirs. Peggy Michel and I had a 7–5 doubles win over Billie Jean and Julie Anthony, who had been unbeaten in twenty-one matches.

Mr. and Mrs. Edwards and I took an apartment in Pittsburgh, and they traveled with the team. Mr. Edwards was general manager, but he was also on the bench helping Ken Rosewall coach the team, and that made it go smoother, so that Ken could concentrate mainly on his own playing. After a few weeks I realized I didn't hate WTT any more. I was beginning to enjoy it, and so was everybody else for the most part. We had a happy team—of course we were winning—

and it got better as we began to know each other and work together. That was the best part, the team spirit. We were in it together, and we were helping each other.

I was astonished at the way we all pulled together. Vitas Gerulaitis and Gerald Battrick had reputations as bad-tempered, uncooperative types, but as members of our team they couldn't have fitted in better. I grew quite fond of them. They were always ready to practice with the women as well as the men, and it was interesting the way our team spirit carried over. At Wimbledon and Forest Hills, we made it a point to watch our teammates' matches and encourage them. I never took such an interest in other players' matches before.

We became used to the outbursts of the spectators, and I think the experience actually helped my concentration. You just shut out everything, even the bench-jockeying by your opponents. That part soured some of the players. Gentlemanly Manolo Santana, who came out of retirement to be player-coach of the New York Sets, was saddened by taunts from the particularly vocal Cleveland bench. He said, "I accept that the spectators will shout and jeer. That is part of what WTT stands for. They pay to come in. But it hurts me when my fellow players who I've known for years say unkind things to me when I'm playing. We players are a brotherhood. We shouldn't insult each other."

But it happened. When Rosewall questioned an umpire's decision once, Billie Jean yelled, "Sit down, you little punk!" Ken looked as though he'd been mugged. He seemed so forlorn that she ran up and threw her arms around him. But another time Ken—yes, the placid, venerable Rosewall—nearly punched young Buster Mottram when Buster's remarks from the Philadelphia bench got to him. Mike Estep of Toronto-Buffalo and Cliff Richey of Cleveland went at each other after Estep, who was playing, traded barbs with Cliff and his sister, Nancy Gunter, who were on the sidelines.

A lighter aspect of bench-jockeying occurred whenever we'd play Philadelphia. Fred Stolle of the Freedoms and Mr. Edwards would needle each other good naturedly. They were old friends, and Fred was one of Mr. Edwards's most successful pupils. "Serve doesn't look too good, Fred," Mr. Edwards would say, just as Fred was tossing the ball.

"Can you fix it up, boss?" Fred would reply.

"Just throw it further out to the left"—which was all wrong.

Despite the travel, we preferred playing on the road. Opposition from the home crowds made us more determined. At home when we'd miss a shot, the people took it so hard. They groaned a lot. They were really behind us, and we didn't want to let them down.

A match we won from Toronto-Buffalo shows how exciting WTT can be. We finally won, 26–25, but nothing could have been dicier. It went down to the very last point of an overtime session. Bear in mind that the team score is cumulative. In the opening set, I beat Wendy Overton, 6–2, so we were ahead by four. In the next set, men's singles, Tom Okker beat Rosewall, 7–5, cutting our lead to two, 11–9. Then Peggy Michel and I beat Laura Rossouw and Jan O'Neill 6–3 in our doubles, putting Pittsburgh ahead, 17–12. We lost the men's doubles, Rosewall and Battrick to Okker and Estep, 7–6, but were still ahead by four, 23–19, going into the final set, mixed doubles. This meant all Michel and Battrick had to do was take three games from Overton and Estep and we'd be out of reach. For Toronto-Buffalo, their only chance was to win it 6–1 or 6–0 to gain a clear victory or 6–2 to pull into a tie. Overton and Estep were fired up and they won the set 6–2, which threw us into a tie, 25–25. Everybody in the place was up and screaming, and they stayed that way through a hairy overtime: a best-of-nine-point sudden-death tie-breaker between the mixed doubles teams. Our side won it, on the last point, 5–4, and the match went to us, 26–25. At 4–4 it was match point for both teams —total chaos and a lot of fun. Maybe it wasn't tennis—as the purists objected—but I couldn't imagine anything more thrilling on a tennis court. And we'd done it as a team.

WTT isn't established by any means, but I think it's here to stay. It all depends on how long the owners can stomach low attendance and huge losses while the public gets tuned in. The average loss was $300,000 per franchise in 1974. There may be fewer teams and a shorter schedule in 1975. I think it had a definite appeal to sports fans who like to follow a home team, who want to see a result, win or lose, when they show up for a match. It's not like going to a tournament and, say, seeing a couple of quarter-final matches one evening. That's all right for a tennis fan, but the general sports fan wants a result: Did Pittsburgh win or lose? Our fans became very fiercely attached to us, more so than fans are to individuals, it seemed.

Mr. Edwards has agreed to coach the Triangles in 1975. Rosewall, at forty, is cutting down his playing and may not return. If he does, he'll be a player only. I still have reservations about WTT, but I'll be back. One factor influencing me is that I've received so many letters from Pittsburgh people encouraging me. The city had no tennis tradition. Ours was the first major tennis to be played there. We made a lot of converts, and being in on something like this from the beginning is quite a kick.

Although he's acted as my manager, handling all my affairs until we signed with International Management, Inc. (an American agency primarily for athletes), Mr. Edwards has never taken a penny of my earnings. He'd be more than justified to extract a percentage from my prize money as International Management does from everything I earn. I'm sure many people believe he does take his cut. He'd be entitled, if only to get something back from all he's spent on me. But does a father cut a daughter? Maybe some do.

I do pay his traveling expenses when he's with me, which is a business expense on my part, taken into account in my income tax return. I also paid him back the money he advanced me to make my first journey to Europe and Britain in 1970. There were no strings attached, but I did win the amount he advanced me in prize money.

Mr. Edwards isn't vague about money as I am. He's meticulous in keeping our books, conscious of every dollar, but only because that's his nature. Everything he does is well ordered. I don't think he's done any more or less for me than he would for any of his other five girls.

He tells his friends, "There was a job to be done with Evonne, and I've done it the best I can, regardless of criticism from some people outside the family circle who don't know us and don't understand."

He believes the job is almost done. It was a five-year plan that he had, although he didn't state it that way when we first came away from Australia in 1970. "She'll win Wimbledon in 1974 and be number one in the world," he said. "By 1974 she will be in full control of her mental and physical powers. She'll be on her own then, able to handle her own affairs with the help of International Management. The travel will be getting a little hard for Eva and me by then, but we'll go with her whenever she wants."

Some people will say, "About time." These are critics in the tennis world who have felt the Edwardses have overprotected me, done too much for me, made me less self-reliant. I've never looked at it that way. To me it's been a family effort. I'll miss them tremendously when they no longer travel with me. I know I can get along, but this has been one of the joys of tennis for me—having someone along that I know, taking a piece of home with me wherever I go. I see players who are so lonely on the circuit, and I think how lucky I've been.

Peggy Michel, an American I've played doubles with and who won Wimbledon in 1974, told me, "There's plenty of time to be off on your own, Evonne. It happens soon enough. In a way you've been on your own since you were thirteen anyway. It's demanding enough just to play tennis, and the Edwardses make it possible to concentrate on that without worrying about too many other details. Why do you think Billie Jean King has a personal traveling secretary? This way you can get the most from your talent. Margaret Court has Barry along as buffer, husband, and baby-sitter. You've got Vic and Eva. You're lucky."

I think so, too.

Back at Wimbledon, Mr. Edwards had just lit another cigarette when I glanced up at the box where he and Mrs. Edwards were sitting it out. Every game had gone to deuce, and I'd won all three. Across the net, Margaret looked a little anxious. Then I lifted the ball above my head, released it like a dove, and took a swing at it just when it seemed the dove might fly away. Crash. Good serve, which Margaret didn't return.

An easy game, this one; for a change I was serving smoothly and gliding in for the volley. Another point, and another. She got one. Then I got the last, winning it at 15. Four games in lights, on the scoreboard, for me. None for Margaret Court. I had more games than any of her five opponents en route to the final, except Judy Tegart, who had managed seven.

I was starting to feel a little sorry for Margaret. I like her. I idolize her. Sure, I wanted to beat her, but I didn't want to humiliate her. Wasn't she going to get a game somewhere?

Not from me, though. No matter how I felt I wasn't going to give her a game. I may lose my concentration or momentum, appear to be sleepwalking, but I'm quite sure I'm always trying. I got very upset with Mr. Edwards after the final of the National Clay Court championships at Indianapolis in 1972 where Chris Evert beat me, 7–6, 6–1. He said I'd stopped trying after losing the first set. I can't say I played well. In fact I played pretty stupidly. Chris lulled me into playing her game. Instead of attacking, I got cautious and stayed on the baseline. So did she, but that's her game, and she chewed me up. That's the first time we'd played on clay, and I wasn't quite sure what to do. But I should have figured about halfway through the set that I might as well go down shooting. I was getting nowhere from the baseline, so I should have gone to the net. I thought I should try to put some pressure on her, even if I did lose. Well, I didn't, and he thought I'd given up. I've never given up, and I always try, and I didn't think he should have told people that I did. We have our fallings-out, just like anybody else, and that was one of them.

If Margaret was going to get some games from me, she'd have to do it on her own. She has a big lifetime edge on me—12–3 in our matches at the close of 1974—and most of the time she's been the better player. She's older, stronger, more experienced. But I know I lost some of those matches because I was awed. I felt strange out on the court saying to myself, "What am I doing here in a match with Margaret? I don't belong here."

"I'm afraid," Mr. Edwards has said, "Evonne's lifelong admiration for Margaret affects her tennis when she plays Margaret. I don't know if she'll get over it. That's no problem with any player but Margaret. Although she's admired Billie Jean King, Evonne hasn't let that admiration get in the way. But she's much closer to Margaret. Margaret has been both a model and a helper."

True enough. But those feelings weren't with me at 4–0 in the first set. Maybe the occasion of Centre Court and a Wimbledon final blotted out the awe. Maybe I was gripped by a quality that people have always said I needed badly: the killer instinct.

I remember once when Mr. Edwards was exasperated with me, he shouted, "Can't you hate her, honey? Can't you get mad at that girl? During the match anyway? She's mad at you. She'd do anything to beat you. If you only had the killer instinct . . ."

But I don't. It's only a game.

Later, when somebody asked Mr. Edwards about this deficiency of mine, he answered, "Well, she won Wimbledon without the killer instinct. You can't do better than that, can you?"

Now it was Margaret's serve. Trouble again. More trouble—for her. A lot of long rallies in this game and pretty soon I was up to break point again, at 15–40. Two break points. One point from a 5–0 lead.

I looked up at my friends. Mrs. Edwards was more dangerous than ever. Her elbows, as I've said, are surgical, but she'd started knitting. With two needles and two elbows she'd be murder if I started to lose.

I couldn't see Barry Court's face. Just the top of his head. Double break point, and he couldn't bear to watch. I didn't blame him.

Margaret was grim. In came the serve, a steamer. I didn't get it back—30–40. Still break point. If I could get this point, I'd be serving for a love set. That would be too incredible . . . and it didn't happen. Back and forth the ball went, and then Margaret came to the net on a ball that I'd hit short. They call her "The Arm" on the tour, and that searching right arm was there to block a volley crosscourt. Deuce. We fought hard for the next four points. Up, back, lobs, smashes, corner to corner. And she won three of them and the game.

For the first time, as we changed ends at 4–1 for me, the applause belonged to Margaret. It gushed loudly over her, and I hope it made her feel better. They were for me all the way, but nobody wanted to see Margaret Court embarrassed. Defeated, but not destroyed.

Later a reporter told me that this game, which removed the o and gave Margaret a 1 on the board, had consumed fifteen minutes. A quarter of an hour fighting off an avalanche, and she made it.

But it was still 4–1 to me, and it was time to put the avalanche back in gear.

Sometimes I wonder what it was that brought Vic Edwards and Evonne Goolagong together. I've described the circumstances, but was it all "meant to be," as Mrs. Edwards believes?

"I believe," she says, "that Evonne was put here to play tennis, to become a champion, and be an inspiration to the Aborigines, to help them. And I believe that Vic was put here to lead her, to help her accomplish these things."

Maybe she's right. She thinks God works like that, and possibly it's so. I'm not a very religious person. Mrs. Edwards and her children are Catholics. Mr. Edwards is Church of England, and so am I, but whenever I go to church, it's mass with Mrs. Edwards and the girls. The first time, years ago, I unsettled them a bit when the congregation was reciting the Lord's Prayer. The Anglican version is longer than the Catholic, and when they'd finished I kept going in a loud voice, oblivious to the fact that everybody else had finished. Suddenly it occurred to me that I was the only one in the church still speaking. I shut up, but Trisha and Jenifer were giggling at me, and I began to laugh, too. Mrs. Edwards had quite a time quieting us down. After that, I learned their version.

It's impossible for me to picture Mr. Edwards as a choir boy, but he was. His mother kept urging him to "be the best" at whatever he did, and he continues as a perfectionist—but an understanding one. He has a soft heart beneath a gruff drill sergeant's exterior, but it takes a while before you find it.

I was nine that first time I met him in Barellan, and he seemed very old then. Yet he seems to have stayed about the same age. An outdoor life is etched on his face, a stern, tough face of a man used to running the show with no ifs, ands, or buts. Until he smiles. The smile is broad, cordial, a "let me shout [buy] you a beer, mate" smile.

His young manhood was spent in the bush, on cattle and sheep properties. It was a rough, invigorating life—on the land, as we say —and if things had worked out as he wished he would be running a cattle property today. Tennis wasn't his idea of a career, maybe because he got so much of it as Herbert Edwards's son. If I had to leave home, the Edwardses' house was an ideal place for a country girl.

I've heard the term "benevolent dictator," and I guess Mr. Edwards would qualify. He is very sure of the way he wants things done, but he knows when to stop pushing, when you just can't go along, or when you need rest. He's been very conscious of when I've had enough tennis, and he's stood up firmly to people who've tried to bend us—to get us to play "just this one more tournament." After I won Wimbledon in 1971, he announced that I wouldn't be playing in the United States, that I'd had enough pressure tennis, and that I wasn't ready for America.

His statements were both ridiculed and knocked in America. I can understand the promoters of Forest Hills wanting the Wimbledon champion in the U.S. Open. It's almost axiomatic that a leading player will be in both. But Rod Laver, for instance, didn't play Forest Hills in 1971, nor did Ken Rosewall, even though he was the defending champion. They'd had enough tennis and needed a rest, and they were old enough and wise enough to know it. So had I, and Mr. Edwards knew it. He suspected I wouldn't like New York, and he was right. And he knew that if I was tired—on top of not being happy in a place —it would be pointless for me to play anyway.

Decisions of this nature on my behalf have annoyed a lot of people—promoters, the press, even some of the tennis public who've wanted to see me play. "Let them be mad at me, honey," he says. "I'll handle it." He's blunt and straightforward and frequently that rubs people the wrong way. There's charm in the man, but you may not come across it for a while. If he's there to say "no" to you, you probably won't encounter it at all. This is the manner he developed in the bush, when he rode for hundreds of miles and scores of days leading cattle drives, and in the Australian army in World War II, when he ascended from private to major.

He's accustomed to giving orders and having them obeyed. When he first meets you, he's cautious, and—if the meeting concerns me— protective. He was that way with all his girls. A young man appearing to take out one of the Edwards girls, or me, gets a close going over. The boy doesn't get a chance to say much. We all resented that. Asking him permission to go out wasn't always easy. Trisha finally stopped asking and went anyway. She was old enough to get away with it, and so am I.

He's like any father. He doesn't want to lose any of us. Five of his girls are gone, and now there's me. I know he's a little jealous of the time I spend with boys, and we have a blow-up about that now and again. He hasn't approved of many I've dated. I can understand that. He's worried that I'll fall in love and let my tennis go, or that I'll get married before I fulfill all our plans. It's a natural feeling on his part, but I know that when it does happen, he'll graciously give me his blessing. Mr. Edwards expects a lot of me—and of himself in guiding me—but he's reasonable and good.

The rock music that I play all the time on the radio or the tape machine drives him up the wall. He hates it, but he accepts that's what people my age like. And he'll accept it when I want to settle down and devote myself to a man and a family rather than tennis. I don't think I could mix the two the way Margaret Court has done so well. (Marriage and a child improved her tennis.) Anyway, I'm not ready for any serious commitments that would take me away from tennis. I'm very content with my life right now.

Mr. Edwards drives himself harder than he does anyone under him. He's had one vacation in his life: a week seventeen years ago after he'd had a heart attack. But with the way he pushes himself, I'm worried about him having another. He's never without a cigarette. About sixty a day is his intake. He'll keep up drink for drink—any drink—with anybody and remain clear in his mind and firm on his feet. His only relaxation is an evening visit to the Mad Corner when he's home. Just before dinner he'll slip away to the Corner, a section of the men's bar at the Willoughby Hotel where he and his mates gather to insult each other and have a few schooners of the Australian ambrosia. One of the regulars at the Mad Corner is Arthur Huxley. Hux, a fine player before the war, heads the tennis division of Slazenger, a sporting goods house, and has been very helpful in my career.

"Where to next, Vic?" Hux will say.

"Japan. We're playing Tokyo and Osaka . . ."

"What a life for you, Vic, all those Geisha girls," one of the others will chime in. "You're damned lucky Evonne needs somebody to go along and carry her rackets."

No women are allowed or wanted at the Mad Corner, a plain, undistinguished bar tiled in white, a place dear to me although I've never entered it. It's a conversational reference point, a hangout for several businessmen whose little favors here and there have helped me on the way up, and a retreat from family and business for Mr. Edwards.

Mr. Edwards doesn't sleep much. If he isn't on the court, he's on the phone making arrangements for me or hard at his paperwork, checking the reports of his staff. On the road it's the same, with the added burden of writing his bulletin, a daily account of me and his other pupils on tour. This is duly mimeographed and distributed by his incomparable secretary, Barbara Worthington, to interested friends, ex-pupils, and reporters he trusts (everything in the bulletin is off the record). Several thousand people read the bulletin and share Mr. Edwards's frustration every time I go walkabout.

I don't know how he keeps up the pace, except that he loves it. He can't sit doing nothing for very long. It's rare that he'll sit through an entire match. Five times he's captained Australian national teams

I've played on: Federation Cup in 1973–74 (a worldwide team competition for women similar to Davis Cup for men); and the Bell Cup in 1972–73–74 (a team match between Australian and American women). We won four of them. As captain, he sat in a chair at courtside to advise us at the change games. This is quite different from the usual tournament situation where a player is on his or her own and no coaching is permitted.

Mr. Edwards had to stay in his chair throughout the matches, an ordeal for him. No greater love could Victor Edwards have for his country than to station himself in the captain's chair for hours and not sneak away once for a beer.

If you're serious about tennis, you need self-discipline. You set aside a so-called normal life and follow the airline and tournament timetables. It's an individual game, and you're on your own. Nobody to substitute for you, nobody to help you out when you get tired, nobody to practice for you. Trisha got sick of it after our first year abroad, 1970. "That's enough," she said. "I've seen London and Paris and Hong Kong and some of the other places. I've had it. No more running for planes, staying in at night because we have to play the next morning, and playing every day whether or not I feel like it. I'll play socially at home, at the club, and enjoy it. I can't take the rat race any more."

So she got off.

"But Evonne," Trisha says, "you enjoy it. You're always looking forward to the next place, the next tournament, the way you looked forward to the Saturday night picture show in Barellan." (That was before television came in and the movie house closed down.) "You don't mind all the flights. You go to sleep as soon as you fasten your seat belt anyway." True enough. "For me it was a grind. I'd rather just catch the bus and go to work every day."

People ask me if I mind the constant travel. Some people, like Trisha, go to work on the bus. I go on the plane. I don't mind. I'm lucky. Trisha says, "Tennis is your life—it's you, Evonne—you'll never quit." I don't look forward to quitting. I don't think about it. I think it's a long way off. Dorothea Lambert-Chambers, who won

95

Wimbledon in 1903, was back in the final in 1920 at age forty-two. May Sutton Bundy—who's still playing, by the way—won Wimbledon in 1905 and was ranked No. 5 in America in 1928 when she was forty-one. Margaret Osborne duPont was forty in 1946 when she was No. 5 in America. I'll be around for a while.

Mr. Edwards has been around in tennis longer than he could have imagined, nearly forty years. He helped his dad out for a while at the courts and worked as an errand boy at Slazenger. But after recovering from a severe case of typhoid fever, he decided to go "out to the scrub," starting as a jackeroo. He moved up to overseer on a property of just on a million acres. He was in the country two years, returned home to help out with the school when old Mr. Edwards got sick, then got back to the land as quickly as he could. After six years he thought he was going to get into a partnership in a property, but that fell through, and he decided to try coaching at Lismore, in the north of New South Wales. Three pounds a week was his retainer. Just before World War II his dad moved on to Western Australia, and Mr. Edwards took over the school. He'd married Mrs. Edwards, and she and his Mum kept the school going during his five years in the army.

Despite his love for the country, Mr. Edwards couldn't deny he had a feeling for teaching. He may have preferred the solitude of the open range, a horse beneath him, and a few trusted hands at his command, but he found his destiny in the country's largest city, and in large cities of the world.

But always outdoors. The wind and sun have chiseled away at his face. His hair is turning silver, his mustache too, but in his seventh decade he walks with spring and sureness. You like him or you don't. He likes you or he doesn't. There's no pulling punches. He says what he thinks, which reporters like very much—unless he says to a reporter, "I'm not talking to you after the way you handled that last story." Mr. Edwards's opinions make lively reading, although they can also bring abuse down on him. But he's too strong inside and out for whatever the opposition may be.

He has pride in his profession—he championed open tennis and honest professionalism by the players well before it became fashion-

Serving at home. I pour tea for my mum and dad, and my seven brothers and sisters.

Wearing the old school tie at Willoughby High School for Girls in Sydney.

A teeny-bopper of serves. I was thirteen, had moved to Sydney and
was beginning my series study with Vic Edwards.
COURTESY OF VIC EDWARDS

First meeting with the idol I'd later beat at Wimbledon. Margaret Court was already a Wimbledon champion. I was thirteen.

Overseas for the first time. In England with Trisha and Mr. Edwards.

Not exactly overjoyed, Billy Jean misses out on a Wimbledon final for the first time in six years after I beat her in the semis of 1971.

Flying and winning in my favorite place—Centre Court, Wimbledon.
I've won the first four games in the 1971 final against Margaret Court.

Eva can't believe it, Vic can't sit, Barry Court can't look during the final at Wimbledon.

MONTE FRESCO, *DAILY MIRROR*

Triumphal recessional. Margaret Court, referee Mike Gibson and the gold platter accompany me from Centre Court following my Wimbledon victory. I was nineteen, both happy and sad about beating my childhood heroine, but mostly happy.

ARTHUR COLE

First tango for Sydneysiders. The band at Wimbledon played "Tie Me Kangaroo Down" as John Newcombe led me through the traditional opening dance by the champions. We were the first Australian couple to share this dance.

PRESS ASSOCIATION LTD.

Chasing an out-of-bounds ball at the Maureen Connolly Brinker
Tennis Tournament in 1973. I was runner-up to Virginia Wade.

A good laugh with my coach, Vic Edwards, at our court in Sydney.

A wet neckerchief helps combat the hottest Forest Hills ever in 1973.

Another serve on the way at Forest Hills, 1973.   JOHN RUSSELL

A solid forehand during my run to the U.S. Open Finals in 1973.
JOHN RUSSELL

My best—a backhand. JOHN RUSSELL

able in Australia—and he has led in establishing standards for the country's teaching professionals, founding the New South Wales Lawn Tennis Professionals Association and the Lawn Tennis Professionals Association of Australia.

If this is starting to seem like an advertisement for Vic Edwards, I guess maybe it is. Where would I be without him? Out in the bush. But where would he be without me? Less burdened. Still running the school, but probably not traveling the world circuit. Of course, I've made his name as much as he's made mine. I'm a justification of his methods and life, I know. And I'm pleased, proud, and lucky to be that.

Mr. Edwards thought a lot about the Aborigines who worked for him. He has told friends, "I was convinced that these dark men we treated as inferiors could be brought up to our standard through education and understanding. I worked with them. I knew their capabilities and as human beings they were equal to the white man. But they have to catch up. I believe it's the duty of white Australians to work with them and help them catch up."

As for me, Mr. Edwards felt there was a job to be done. "We brought her into our home and raised her as we raised our natural daughters, and you see the result."

Was this a certain missionary zeal? Are quotes like that patronizing, condescending? Paternalistic? Some Aborigines would say so. "They've [the Edwardses] filled her with the white man's values, cut her off from her people," says one of my Aboriginal friends, a university graduate. "She's more white than black."

I'm aware of that sort of criticism. It hurts, but I don't regret a day with the Edwardses. They made it possible for me to refine whatever talent I had, to show that an Aborigine could make it to the top of a profession. The Edwardses' outlook wouldn't coincide with that of the young militant Aborigines. It couldn't. Age and background are against it.

All I know is when someone reached out to me with love and understanding, I took hold.

97

I'll never forget that face: hard, made-up, arching eyebrows. I think her partner called her Marion, but that doesn't matter. It's what she shouted: "Nigger!"

Nigger? Neither Trisha nor I had ever heard the word. Sometimes people use it to refer insultingly to Aborigines, but it's not common. I'd heard "boong," which is more common, more insulting —but I'd never heard it directed at me. I'd never had any racial problems. Growing up as the only Aborigines in Barellan, we were poor, but fully accepted or so we felt. We had fights with the neighborhood kids, the same fights kids have everywhere. And we made up and were good friends. Color had nothing to do with the fights or the friendships. We were just kids.

Still, when Mr. Edwards discussed my coming to Sydney with Mr. Kurtzman he brought up the potentially explosive fact of color. He said to Mr. Kurtzman, "Bill, you must realize that she may be snubbed in women's tennis. They can be a bitchy lot, and they're having their problems now."

The leading women, including Margaret Court, were fighting with our administrators of the game, the Lawn Tennis Association of Australia, and as usual, the women were getting the short end. They had no representation, no one to speak out for them and obtain fairer treatment. Even in this somewhat liberated era, not one woman holds office in the LTAA, and national women's teams are selected by an all-male panel!

"You know how it is with women," Mr. Edwards said. "The older ones don't make it easy for a newcomer, and if that newcomer is an Aborigine . . . well . . . it's something to consider before you send her away with me."

If it was something to consider, I never knew about it. I wasn't snubbed, maligned, or discriminated against. Sometimes people tried to be so nice they were unnatural. I've mentioned that the publicity I got was more than my due. I was awed by it at first, then I wished it would go away until I lived up to it, by which time I wouldn't pay any attention anyway. Sometimes I read what's written about me, but not often. I've wondered more than once whether a twenty-three year old has lived enough to rate an autobiography.

By the time I was sixteen, I'd played hundreds of matches in Sydney without anything untoward happening, other than a very occasional loss, and the "first Aborigine" stuff was pretty much forgotten. I was better known, but I was just one of many promising teen-agers in the city, playing as much as I could in a variety of competitions, team and individual.

Trisha and I played for White City in a women's interclub league. This was on grass, a surface I took to right away when I came to Sydney. There's nothing as delightful underfoot as a good grass court. Grass suits my attacking game, and I suppose it's my best surface, although by this time I feel at home on anything.

We were playing two "old women"—I suppose they were in their thirties—and beating them, and they didn't like it. Maybe we weren't on our best behavior either. In matches we were certain to win, Trisha and I tended not to pay too much attention. We'd forget the score and dawdle about. It isn't polite to your opponents. Finally we won and came to the net to shake hands.

Nobody was smiling. The woman I'll always remember glared at me, her eyes fierce beneath those plucked eyebrows. "That's the first time I ever lost to a little nigger," she growled.

Trisha began to cry.

"What are you crying about?" The woman was startled.

"You hurt my sister," Trisha said somehow between sobs.

"She's not your sister!"

"She is my sister, and when you hurt her you hurt me—"

I hadn't been hurt because I'd never heard "nigger" before, but I could tell by the way she said it that the woman was trying to be hateful.

I was crying, too. Not because of what had been said—but because Trisha was crying. We could set each other off very easily. We were bawling loudly, tears streaming down, and people on other courts had stopped their games and were looking over at us, wondering what was going on. Our opponents walked off, but we were still there weeping madly.

99

The captain of our team came over and asked what had happened. We couldn't stop crying. We wouldn't have told her anyway because we didn't really understand what had happened. Up to the changing room we went, still bawling. These matches had always been a lot of fun, quite social, with a party for the visiting team when the tennis was completed. Our captain came into the changing room and asked us to come down to the party. "We've got a chocolate cake, Evonne," she said, knowing that was my favorite food. More sobs. She gave up. If chocolate cake couldn't stop the flood, nothing would.

At last we took our showers and got dressed. I had an appointment somewhere and went off. Trisha went home and told Mrs. Edwards about what had happened. After a while they wondered where I was. Trish had forgotten where I'd gone, and when I didn't come home, she started to cry again, "Evonne's gone back to Barellan. She's gone and won't live with us any more because of what happened."

About then I walked in the door. Trisha was still crying, so I started again. We were hugging each other and wailing while Mrs. Edwards shook her head.

Mr. Edwards was very upset when he heard about it, and so were the people at that woman's club. An apologetic phone call came from the club president, who said the woman would never again play for their team. She didn't. The story didn't get out to the newspapers, and everybody in the two clubs tried to forget it. White City said they would never play again if the offending woman was on the team. But she was soon gone from the club altogether, informed that she would no longer be welcome, I later heard. It didn't concern me that much. I didn't want a personal apology or a chance to get back at her— nothing like that. I was more stunned than hurt, and it probably would have gone right by me if Trisha hadn't begun to cry. But I was very touched when Trish said, "You've hurt my sister, and when you hurt my sister you hurt me."

I'll probably never see that woman again, but if I do, I'll know her. Hers is a face I won't forget.

Trisha is a girl I can cry with. I don't know why, but when one of us cries it triggers the other one to sob along.

We never cried over tennis. Cry over a game? The first tournament I ever played in America, the Maureen Connolly Brinker International in Dallas, the winter of 1972, Chris Evert and I were both beaten by Billie Jean King. The tournament promoters were hoping to present the opener in the Evert-Goolagong rivalry, but Billie Jean got to us before we could get at each other, Chrissie in the quarters, me in the semis.

Chrissie led Billie Jean all through the match, but lost 7–5 in the third, dropping the last three games. I went into the locker room to change for a doubles match, and there was Chrissie bawling her eyes out. I didn't know her—we'd just met a day or so before—and I didn't say anything. There wasn't anything to say; I was embarrassed. I never know what to say to somebody who's taking a loss so hard. I can't understand it. I thought, "I hope I never come to this." I don't think I will. I'll know something's wrong if I do. Games aren't something to cry over.

But is that any sillier than crying over a movie? Trisha and I were always doing that. A sad movie on television would kill us. We'd sit in the living room howling and dripping, and Mr. Edwards would say, "Too bad you can't get that serious about your tennis." But he knew we couldn't. He was resigned to that.

On our first big trip, when we went overseas in 1970, Trisha began sniveling when the plane took off from the Sydney airport, and we were into an all-out weep before we were a hundred feet off the ground.

"I'm going to miss everybody so much," she wept.

I was anxious to go, but she was my sob sister and I responded in the usual way.

So did Mr. Edwards: "What in the world's wrong with you girls? You've wanted to go on this trip for a couple of years . . . oh, well."

We cried all the way to Singapore, which may have been a distance record.

It was the same old Trisha when I won Wimbledon in 1971. She was at home in Sydney, watching on television—and crying all the way. If it had gone three sets, she might have permanently disabled her tear ducts.

Sometimes I'd hear her crying in a high octave, "Evonne, come here quick and get this bug!"

Trisha and Jenifer are deathly afraid of insects. For some reason I became the hit woman, the dispatcher of disagreeable creatures.

"We thought," says Trisha, "that Evonne being from the country and having done all that hunting and fishing with her brothers, she'd know what to do with these frightful things that were always turning up."

Spiders, moths, crickets, they sent me after each of these invaders with a broom. I went unbeaten against all of them. Nobody can stay with me when I'm swinging a broom. A little topspin and it's good-bye spiders.

Who says I don't have the killer instinct?

It was two o'clock the following morning in Barellan when Margaret Court and I began our 1971 Wimbledon final, and by 2:00 A.M. on any other day Barellan would have been tucked in and faster asleep than a hibernating bear. However, that early morning of July 3, lights shone in every window in town. Everybody was up watching Margaret and me on television, which was beaming into Australia by satellite.

There was a party at the War Memorial Club, with a lot of barracking (cheering) for me every time I got a point. In that barroom the only decorations are the television set and a photo of Queen Elizabeth.

At my house there was also a party for the family and some neighbors. Fish and chips, beer, and soft drinks. The kids were bedded down on the floor of the living room, in front of the telly, and they were all barracking, too. "Come on, Goolie!" was the cry. Mum was nervous. She has high blood pressure, and an occasion such as this was not recommended treatment.

"I don't know if I can stand it," she said to Dad.

"I may have a beer," he said.

I was about to have a bit of strife from Margaret. Serving at 4–1 instead of 5–0 because I'd let two break points get away, I let up just a little. I didn't pay as close attention as I should have on my first serve, and it started to miss. This was what Margaret was waiting for, and she stepped in to take my second serve, moving right to the net behind her return. That's a tactic she and Billie Jean King use very productively against me. It's the way the game should be played, but very few women are able to do it: attack your opponent's second serve and put the pressure on her. When I'm playing well I can do it, and I have to do it to beat Chris Evert—knock her off balance before she can get set at the baseline.

So Margaret began her move and she broke me quite easily at 15, to retrieve one of the service breaks and come closer at 2–4.

"Don't like that very much," Mrs. Edwards muttered.

Barry Court was able to look up at the scoreboard.

Dad took a long gulp of beer.

Trisha in Sydney reached for another tissue and whimpered harder.

As the plane carrying Trisha and me headed for Singapore, in March of 1970, I knew this was what I'd been preparing for over the years, since I'd read the comic book about the girl winning Wimbledon. "Coming away" is the expression Australian tennis players use. You don't know if you can become a world-class player until you come away from Australia and get out into the world of Wimbledon, Forest Hills, Roland Garros, and Foro Italico.

We'd talked about it for years, and now we were heading out there from Singapore to Britain and Europe. When you leave Australia, you just don't pop back every so often to see the folks and friends. It's too far, even in the era of the jet. You leave early in the year, and you come back months later, like the sailors in the old days of clipper ships. We departed in March and returned early in September. Nearly six months on the road. Not an unusual tour for an Australian. Baseball, basketball, or hockey players talk about long road trips and mean two or three weeks, but they don't know what a road trip is. Try packing for a six-month trip some time and not exceeding the airline weight limits.

Our travels up until then had been relatively short. Drives of six and seven hours out into the country had been the longest. Mostly we'd traveled by car. Now it would be planes. Country roads? We'd sped and bumped along all kinds including the "Crystal Highway," a one-lane track between Nevertire and Nyngan that got its name from all the shattered "crystal" along the way. Wheeling along and sighting an infrequent car coming at you head-on, you pull onto a gravel shoulder—as does the oncoming vehicle—precipitating a shower of rocks that doesn't do any good for a windshield.

Tennis can't be any more fun than it was when Mrs. Edwards lugged Trisha and me around to those country tournaments. As I perfect my game and learn to do more things with a racket, as I approach my peak and play for larger crowds, I suppose there's more satisfaction. But for sheer fun and giggles, kids' tennis is hard to beat.

At Bathurst, which calls itself the "Queen City of the Western Plains," we often played in track suits and gloves because it was June —our winter—and it was cold in the morning and at night. We'd start at 9:00 A.M., and sometimes there'd be a fog on the courts so you could hardly see your opponent. The ball would shoot out of the fog where you didn't expect it, and the match would become a guessing game until the mist slid away. One day I played twenty-six sets there, from nine in the morning until midnight. I went to bed giggling from fatigue, but I was up eager the next day.

All sorts of courts—antbed, gravel, loam, asphalt, concrete. Good, bad, level, bumpy, uphill, downhill . . . none as luxurious as the grass of Sydney.

Antbed is Australia's own special country surface, white or red, depending on the anthills in that territory. You knock down the anthill and spread the grit on a bare patch of ground from which you've skinned the grass. It makes a good court, but we don't have anything as exotic as the dried cowdung courts of India.

Cowra is another country town, not far from Kangaroo Flat,

where we cleaned up on trophies. I won New South Wales Hard Court titles there at a small club amid rolling terrain. These were great occasions for families. They'd bring the children for a weekend excursion, and maybe all the kids in a family would play in the tournament. Janine Murdock, one of my big rivals—I lost only three singles matches between the ages of thirteen and seventeen, and two of them were to Janine—would be watching her kid sisters and brothers out of the corner of an eye while she played. I don't understand how she concentrated. She'd be yelling at them during a match—don't do this, or don't do that. She probably has a family of her own now.

We played in Young, a sizeable town just down the road from Wombat. Once at Young I asked a gas station attendant how far it was to Barellan. "What's Barellan?" he answered.

In one of those finals Trisha and I were playing two local girls. We lost the first set and were behind 5-2 in the second.

"What's the score, Trisha?" I said, my usual attentive self.

"Five–two—and not to us," she looked a little worried. So I shouted "Geronimo! Got to get to the net," and we won five straight games for the set, and then the match.

Mrs. Edwards wasn't amused. "You rotten kids, don't ever do that again! Do you hear?"

"Why? . . . we were all right . . ."

"I'll tell you why—because I'd never have heard the end of it from their mothers. I'd have had to listen to them crowing about that match the rest of my life."

Mrs. Edwards had her spectating problems.

"We never thought we'd lose," I said nonchalantly.

"Well, let us know, Evonne, if you please. Let us in on your secrets," she said.

I try to remember to do that, but most of the time I forget.

You get to the country pretty fast from Sydney, through the Blue Mountains, which are really just hills, where you hear the piercing cry of the bellbirds, sharp and clear. Through the coal-mining town of Lithgow, through small and medium-sized towns that have one thing in common—tennis clubs. Tennis is booming beyond belief in America, far beyond anything happening in Australia, but would you find a tennis club, however humble, in a coal-mining town in the United States?

The Blue Mountains simmer down to rolling, grazing country, washed by purple seas of a weed called Patterson's Curse. An acre will support eight sheep in the area around Cowra, but as you move west toward Barellan, the land slumps disconsolately into flat, dry expanses where the country belongs to wheat, and the sheep have to look harder for a bite. The land isn't hospitable to much more than a head per acre.

This is the "country" I'm always talking about, the bush. But it is not the Outback. That's one of the Goolagong myths—the girl from the Outback. Sportswriters sometimes get carried away, as they did in labeling Ilie Nastase "the Romanian shepherd boy." He retorted, "We've got 2 million people in Bucharest where I grew up, and no sheep."

I'm from the inner country. The Outback is further out, but Barellan is out as far as you'd want to go. I haven't even been to the Outback—most Australians haven't—but I'd like to go someday. There's a lot of my country I want to see. I guess when reporters in other countries started writing about me and learned I was from a sheep-and-wheat town of fewer than 1,000 inhabitants, I had to be from the Outback. So be it.

I'd won just about everything I could win in Australia for my age, all the teen-age, country, district, and state and national championships, and it was time to see what the innocent bushie could do abroad. There was some talk of my going when I was sixteen. Other Australians have come away that young. We talked it over. I wanted Trisha to go, too, and she was finishing school, a year behind me. Then we thought business college would be a good idea for us. So we waited until 1970. "I think that's the year to go," said Mr. Edwards.

And we went, laughing all the way to the airport, and crying all the way to Singapore.

Wimbledon was the place we wanted to play above all, but that was three months in the future, and we didn't expect to do much there anyway. If we were going to make our marks, it would be in the smaller tournaments leading up to the Big W, like Southport.

England. This is where tennis—at least our game of lawn tennis—began officially in 1874 when our founding father, Walter Clopton Wingfield patented a diversion involving rackets, ball, net, and an hourglass-shaped court. The Greeks had a word for it—sphairistike—and Wingfield used it. Thank heavens that didn't stick.

Sphairistike was soon overcome by the term "lawn tennis" (all the courts were grass then), and the Big Daddy of tennis, Walter Wingfield, learned sadly that his patent didn't mean much. Several manufacturers put out tennis equipment, court specifications, and rules. In 1877, the year of the first Wimbledon, the rules were standardized and have changed very little since.

Tennis had existed in various forms prior to Wingfield, dating back to such figures as Henry VIII, perhaps the No. 1 mixed doubles player of all time (although his six partners might not agree with that ranking). King Henry used to take along his own scorekeeper, a fellow named Anthony Angeley, wherever he played. That might have been worth a point or two.

Wingfield didn't make much on his patent, but he has earned his niche in history as the bloke who got lawn tennis going. Despite a terrible climate for the game, English enthusiasm has kept it going on their island as nowhere else. The English public's love and concern for the game and the press's attention to it are beyond what you'll find anywhere, even in America, where there are so many more players and much more money devoted to tennis.

March was dreadful: the worst weather they'd experienced in Southport for years. There we were in our summer dresses and goosebumps, fitting in matches between rain, sleet, and snowstorms. Everybody else was bundled in track suits, which we obtained as soon as possible.

It was the first snow Trisha and I had ever seen, but not enough of it stuck to the ground to build a snowman. That pleasure came three years later when I was caught in a blizzard in Akron, Ohio.

Tennis goes on in England regardless of the elements. Their hard courts, a red shale, can take a lot of soaking. Play started, stopped, and started again. Whenever we could we fled to our old, small hotel to feed shillings to the heater in the room. You had to pay for the heat, a shilling an hour, and we paid gladly. Mr. Edwards had told us food and lodging would be plain when we started out. "But the food will be good—steaks and salads for the most part." We were traveling as reasonably as possible. We hadn't showed that we could pay our way yet. But we never had another hotel where we had to prime the heater with money.

It was a little tricky staying warm and getting used to the slippery British clay, but I broke in at Southport all right, beating Corinne Molesworth (the British under-twenty-one champion) in the semis and Joyce Williams (fifth ranked in Britain) in the final. A hot week in a cold town.

First prize: £40 sterling ($96). Plus £5 as a doubles semifinalist with Trisha. So this was big-time professional tennis? I wasn't aware of the amount until Mr. Edwards told me. But it was the first money I'd earned playing tennis, not a bad feeling.

After the storms and chill of Southport, the prospect of Stalybridge and Poole seemed marvelous. Both tournaments were indoors, a strange phenomenon to Trisha and myself who had played only outdoors. Interesting, but not satisfying. I've played a lot of indoor tennis since, but I don't like it.

Following these two tournaments were a few more in London. The weather was fining up, but it still wasn't our idea of springtime as we moved down to Bournemouth for our first major event, the British Hard Court Championships. The bigger names from around the world were beginning to show up; the tournament would be won by Margaret Court over Virginia Wade.

Blustery winds came in from the sea, and few people took advantage of the boardwalk at the beach. But English spectators are hardy. They turn out heavily for this "Runny Nose Open" at the West Hants Club, a neatly landscaped ground where David Gray, the extremely literate tennis correspondent of the *Guardian*, may be seen sitting in the middle of a rose garden, scribbling his copy before phoning it to London. I see a lot of the London press because they're at most of the big tournaments in Europe and America, and I enjoy them. They travel together, drink together, argue together—and write separately. Mostly men, but I mustn't forget the incredible Judith Elian, a member of the British press group although she actually reports for *L'Equipe* of Paris. The only woman on the staff, she speaks eight or nine languages, talks to each player in his own language, doesn't have too much trouble understanding Australian, and seldom writes about women. She and her readers prefer the men, and if I see Judy in the press stand when I'm playing I know it must be an important match.

Bournemouth is where open tennis began in April of 1968. After too many years of hanging back in the Victorian shadows and perpetuating a phony amateurism, tennis abruptly jumped into the present when the International Lawn Tennis Federation finally approved the mingling of amateurs and the outcast pros at the traditional tournaments, plus the payment of prize money to the pros. Thereafter, nearly every player serious about the game embraced professionalism to get in on the money. Now the only amateurs are pretty much legitimate amateurs, juniors (below age nineteen), or collegians. Of course the Russians and some other communist countries advertise their players as amateurs, too. If they are amateurs, so are the stars of the Bolshoi Ballet.

An Australian pro, Owen Davidson, won the first open match over a Scotsman, amateur John Clifton, to launch the British Hard Courts' plunge into the twentieth century in 1968. That week a curly-headed Englishman, Mark Cox, wrote his footnote in sporting history by beating Pancho Gonzalez and Roy Emerson in succession, the first wins by an amateur over a pro.

When I say tennis came up to date, I actually mean the International Lawn Tennis Federation, the governing body of the game since 1913, which includes the national associations of more than eighty countries. The administrators are all amateurs, volunteers, and it is questionable whether they will continue to govern the prize money game, simply because amateurs and professionals have different goals and outlooks.

Tennis politics is totally confusing now, an alphabet soup seasoned with ILTF; WCT; WTT; VS (Virginia Slims); WTA (Women's Tennis Association, the women's union); ATP (Association of Tennis Pros, the men's union); and the various LTAs (Lawn Tennis Associations, the most important being those of Britain, the U.S., France, and Australia—the Big Four).

Probably no more than a handful of people have a firm grasp of the political situation of day-to-day tennis. It's changing even as I write this sentence. All I—and most of the players—want is to play the game. The tremendous influx of money has naturally made some players greedy. Consider that in 1968, the first year of international prize money tennis (this doesn't count the wayward exhibition tours of the outcasts, limited to a few pros per year between 1926 and 1968), there were only a few hundred thousand dollars available throughout the world for men and women. For the year 1974 the figure was about $7.7 million. Women have made even more startling advances in this short time than the men. Total prize money in female tennis in 1970 was around $100,000; but by 1973 Margaret Court plucked more than $200,000 in tournament earnings; Billie Jean King, Chris Evert, and I were above $100,000; and the total figure was nearly $2 million.

The Virginia Slims circuit slogan proclaims, we've "come a long way, baby," but I doubt that a majority of us are motivated by money. Chris Evert, for example, turned her back on more than $50,000 in prize money during 1972 because she and her parents decided she shouldn't turn pro until her eighteenth birthday, in December of that year.

I'm not even sure Billie Jean thinks much about money. Her crusade has been waged to gain for women the financial attention we warrant during the tennis boom, and I think all female tennis players should be grateful that she's such a forceful advocate. Her demand for equal prize money at major tournaments was at last rewarded at the U.S. Open of 1973 when the victors John Newcombe and Margaret Court each received $25,000. In fact, by beating Bobby Riggs in their gawdy meeting following Forest Hills, Billie Jean won $100,000, and that's the juiciest plum ever in tennis.

Billie Jean's war began in earnest in 1970 in Rome when she learned she was to get only $600 for winning the Italian championship. The $600 didn't bother her so much as the $3,500 that Ilie Nastase got for winning the men's title. "It's ridiculous," she wailed. "The ratio is 6 to 1." What really infuriated Billie Jean was the Pacific Southwest Open at Los Angeles a few months later. The ratio was greater than 8 to 1, a $12,000 first prize for Rod Laver compared to $1,500 for Lesley Hunt. That did it. Eight women with a lot of backbone—Billie Jean, Kerry Melville, Rosie Casals, Nancy Gunter, Judy Dalton, Kristy Pigeon, Peaches Bartkowicz, and Val Ziegenfuss— boycotted the Pacific Southwest and played a quickly organized tournament the same week in Houston. Gladys Heldman, publisher of *World Tennis* magazine and a leader in the women's struggle, talked her friend Joe Cullman, president of Philip Morris, into sponsoring the Houston tourney on behalf of a subsidiary, Virginia Slims cigarettes. Prize money was $9,500 (versus $7,500 at Los Angeles), and winner Casals made $1,700.

However, in opposing the open at Los Angeles, Houston was an outlaw tournament, and the rebels risked suspension by the USLTA. Suspensions did indeed fall, but they were later rescinded. Peace was made (to be broken several times), and the Virginia Slims women made their point: they would no longer play for inferior prize money or be dictated to by the men who operate the USLTA. That was the beginning of the astonishing rise in the growth and popularity of women's pro tennis. Prodded by the rich Virginia Slims circuit, which grew to twenty-eight tournaments worth $775,000 in 1973, and ringleader King, the LTAs had to respond to the women and elevate prize money everywhere. The Slims women also demonstrated with their 1971, 1972, 1973, and 1974 circuits that they could gain more attention and money by divorcing themselves from the men and traveling a separate tournament schedule. "The men," said Billie Jean, "are always going to want more money than us. When we're on our own, all the money and all the publicity goes to us."

I don't agree with everything Billie Jean says. I prefer big tournaments like Wimbledon and the other European tournaments that have both men's and women's events and where we're all together. But there's no denying that she's been a fantastic force in driving our game ahead. By focusing interest on the game itself, Billie Jean has put a lot of money in the pockets of the male players as well. But try to get one of them to admit it!

Something very big, often chaotic and out of control, began in the seaside resort of Bournemouth, April 22, 1968, the birth of open tennis. In short, modern tennis is barely seven years old. When followers of the game get wrought up about all the problems and factions, they ought to be a little more patient. The game has done pretty well in seven years, but it can't all be ironed out perfectly in such a brief time.

I'll leave the sorting out to the unions, the LTAs, the players' agents, those who are commercially oriented. That doesn't mean I won't sign my checks and deposit them, but the politicians, hustlers, and promoters and I are on different wave lengths.

Not that I haven't gotten into the politics of the game—at least by proxy. Near the end of 1971 we decided I'd play a couple of tournaments in New Zealand. Screams of anguish were heard from organizers of tournaments on the Australian circuit. The promoters were saying, "Evonne's Australian. She's got to play in all of our tournaments." They were urging my LTA to bar me from going elsewhere when I could be helping the tournaments at home.

Mr. Edwards responded by pointing out there was little or no prize money in the Australian events. He sent word around that my appearance fee would be $2,500 to play in an Australian tourney. Promoters were aghast. Total prize money for a women's event didn't amount to that much. Well, did they want the Wimbledon champion or not?

Yes they did, and they found the money. Mr. Edwards stated: "It was time they started thinking that the women were worthwhile. Pro tennis was here, and Australia was way behind. It was antiquated to think that a world champion should appear for a pittance when she could earn a worthwhile sum elsewhere. I considered the plight of Australian tennis very carefully before I used Evonne as a lever.

"But when I did, the organizers realized it was time to get up to date. They were compelled to find sponsors to meet the payments to Evonne. That made them look outside their narrow circle and see what was happening elsewhere in the world. By using modern promotional methods and obtaining commercial sponsorship, they were able to offer worthwhile prize money to the women for the leading events on our circuit. But if Evonne hadn't stood fast by her demands, women's pro tennis in Australia would still be very minor."

Still, it was a gamble. The LTAA could have banned me for refusing to play their tournaments. We gambled that they wouldn't be so harsh to a Wimbledon champion over the matter of such a small amount of money, considering the overall world situation. They wouldn't have looked very good. Guarantees, which I received that season in Australia, are against the spirit of open tennis. Payment should be based on results: no win, no earn. Thus we are basically opposed to guarantees. But we felt that in this case it was the only way to bring about reasonable compensation for women in our country.

That's a long way from Bournemouth, yet Bournemouth was the fountainhead. Bournemouth, where Ken Rosewall got $2,400 and Virginia Wade $720 for winning the first open singles.

Bournemouth was also the scene of Ilie Nastase's memorable when-you-gotta-go-you-gotta-go retreat of 1972. At 5–5 in the second set of his semifinal against Bob Hewitt, Nastase, the wild and wondrous Romanian, asked to be excused—he had to go to the bathroom. That's no excuse in tennis. Play is continuous, says a much-abused rule. But the referee, Captain Gibson, undoubtedly recalled that only a few months before, during an indoor tournament in London's Albert Hall, the erratic Ilie departed without asking permission—and didn't return. On that widely heralded occasion, Clark Graebner had stepped across the net and advised Nastase that if he didn't cease his distracting tactics he would receive one of Graebner's best strokes in the nose. Nastase's bickering, grousing, mimicking of his opponents, fits of temper, and generally childish (but sometimes entertaining) deportment tend to annoy his opponents. Graebner threatened violence, and it got Clark an easy win. Nastase, saying "he frightened me," walked away from the match, giving it to Graebner by forfeit.

It's highly irregular for a referee to grant permission for a player to leave the court for any reason while a match is in progress. (Rod Laver recalls his partner, Darlene Hard, suddenly disappearing from the Wimbledon mixed doubles final of 1960 on Centre Court, leaving him and foes Maria Bueno and Bob Howe gaping. Struck unexpectedly by a periodic malady, Darlene fled without a word. Rod shrugged. He, his opponents, and 14,000 customers were mystified. In a few minutes she returned. Rather than default a final, the referee wisely asked no questions and nodded to carry on.) Nastase would probably depart whether permission was granted or not, referee Gibson reasoned, so he agreed to Nastase's request.

While 4,000 in the West Hants stadium waited for Nastase and nature, millions across Britain followed his 100-yard dash to the toilet over television. As Nasty sprinted from the stadium to the clubhouse, the cameras followed every step until he slipped through the door and out of sight.

Relieved but not reprieved, Nasty returned and lost the match.

I knew I was in the big league when I walked around the Bournemouth club. Not only were Court and Wade in the tournament, but so were King, Casals, Heldman, Kerry Melville, Ann Jones, and Winnie Shaw. It would have been hard to find a more spectacular lineup, and enough for me to beat Nell Truman, the No. 6 Briton. But then I knocked over Casals, 6–2, 6–3, and Heldman, 1–6, 6–1, 13–11, and I was in the semis where I had a 4–1 lead on Court in the second set before she said: Enough, child, and whipped me, 6–1, 6–4. "That's the best you've played against me. You're coming along fine," Margaret said.

But it felt better to win over Rosie Casals, who had been a star for a long time although she was only twenty-one at the time. I went onto the court annoyed, unusual for me. I'd heard that Rosie and the other Americans were saying I'd had too much publicity and was overrated, that I'd crumple now that the strong women had appeared. They were right about the publicity—if they had in fact said it. I never found out if they did, but I was a little toey—riled up—and I had a good day against Rosie. She didn't like the slippery clay or the bleak, raw weather, and I was getting used to both. She bounced everywhere, an energetic volleyball, but I was hitting my groundies beyond her churning legs. On match point she came streaming to the net on a forehand drive. I moved in a couple of steps to take the ball before it bounced and turned it into a softly volleyed lob that sailed over her head. I remember Tony Roche standing beside the court and chuckling, "That's a real bushie shot." I smiled. Another bushie can call you a bushie and get away with it. It was nice being noticed by the bushie from Tarcutta who seemed ready to take the world over from Rod Laver until he hurt his shoulder.

I knew Julie Heldman would be tougher than Rosie because Julie can stay out there all day and hit groundstrokes from the baseline. She loves a slow court, and she's as smart as she is steady. I just made up my mind I was going to stay with her until one of us gave way. Up the score went in the third set, and down came the rain. Back and forth went the balls, muddy red clods that felt like bowling balls clunking off our rackets. The rallies were as steady as the rain. But Julie made a few more mistakes than I did, and I won the longest set I've played, 13–11, and a spot in the semis. The Americans were all very complimentary. Now I felt I belonged on the international circuit, and I was not embarrassed by the publicity that week.

I'd won the first four games in that Wimbledon final, but Margaret took the next two, and she was beginning to charge forward, hovering at the net. She seems an octopus in a short skirt, all arms, stretching either way to cut off your best passing shots with strong volleys.

It was her turn to serve, and she was operating with confidence, playing serve-and-volley, whacking the first ball to my backhand, and getting to the net so quickly I thought she was serving from well inside the baseline. You get that feeling when Margaret is on her game. She was calm. She no longer looked harried and that meant she was extra dangerous.

She won her serve fairly easily, to 3–4. More sighs and groans from the crowd. Then she jumped on my serve to push me into a tight corner called 15–40: double break point. One more good swing and she would have completely erased my huge lead. Huge? That was only minutes ago, but a tennis match can change around quicker than you can say double fault—or make one.

One point. It doesn't seem like much, but that's the beauty of tennis scoring. One point in the crisis can mean everything. And this was my first crisis. I'm amused by droll English journalists like Rex Bellamy or David Gray, who will enter the grandstand after a match has begun and whisper to a colleague, "Have I missed the crisis, for heaven's sake?" Or, "Please, don't neglect to tell me when the crisis arrives."

It's an overworked word, especially when applied to a game, but if Margaret had broken me there, I seriously doubt that I could have stopped her because then she would have had that other cliché— momentum—going for her.

I wasn't thinking about weathering crises or immobilizing momentum. I just wanted to put my first serve into play to get the jump on her. Otherwise she'd have a knock at my second and be right up there at the net again, like a traffic cop directing me to get lost.

All right, give 'er a go, mate. I tried to put the serve on her backhand side, close to her body so she wouldn't have too good a swing at it. I was coming to the net myself with it to put the pressure on her. She went down the line with her return, which I reached with a good forehand volley. The ball bounced once . . . twice before she could scoop it. My point.

Thirty-forty. Still break point. I wanted to play serve-and-volley again, but my first serve missed. The edge went to Margaret and she was eager to exploit it. My second serve was okay, and we traded a couple of shots from the baseline before she took advantage of a short ball of mine, near the service line, and pressed forward with a crackling crosscourt forehand. I knew she was guarding the net again, but I didn't see her. No time to look. I was dashing to my right, intent on getting to that ball some way and slapping it back any way. The only way was a lob, a shot I don't use enough. Nobody does. Only the crafty hackers in the public parks seem to understand the true value of the lob. This one was super valuable. I flicked it on the run . . . slight murmur of wonder and approval from the audience . . . managed a little topspin on it . . . and reversed my direction, trying to get back to the court and into position at the midpoint of the baseline. I sneaked a look now. The ball was soaring, and Margaret had reversed, too, about-facing to race to the backcourt.

Too late. The ball bounced and spun away. Good old topspin. I couldn't see where the ball landed. Silence. Lovely silence: no call of "Out!" from the linesman. Explosion of applause, then "Deuce!" from the umpire. I'll try to remember that shot all my life, but I probably won't. Too many shots. Scratch one crisis. I won the next two points on her errors and had a 5–3 lead.

That's a good place to be. She'd have to take four straight games to win the set, and I could win it in either of the next two, by breaking her serve or holding my own.

Where do you learn to hit a lob that will clear even Margaret Court and elude her grasp? In the local wheat silo.

"She's a mighty lass, our Evonne," Red Dicker said to a visitor. "Say a word against her around here and it's like trying to open a clam with a playing card." Later Mr. Dicker, who has lived in Barellan longer than anybody else ("hatched here in 1901"), would say, "That was the night of nights, Evonne, when we stayed up all night to watch you win Wimbledon." He was one of those who contributed to my fund. A great night, but to be objective about it, it wasn't Barellan's greatest moment.

The next time you're in Barellan, drop by Barry Tubb's butcher shop. Just walk along Yapunyah Street, across from the railroad tracks and the silos, beneath the tin canopies that shield the sidewalks from the sun. Yapunyah Street could be a set out of any Hollywood

Western. Without the cars parked in front of the Commercial Hotel, it's Dodge City. Somebody might confront you with, "Guh-dye, myte, 'owzit gun?" But that's merely the native salutation, "Good day, mate, how's it going?"

You'll find Barry Tubb's place without much trouble. Just past Younghusband Ltd., Wool & Produce Brokers, whose broad window is the last word in fashionable display, containing a sack of Fortified Calf Milk Replacer and a couple of barrels of Acmal's No. 1 Mineral and Vitamin Food Supplement for Pigs. Do your Christmas shopping early.

Tubb's is right there, the only butcher shop in town, and quite possibly the only one in the world fronted by a stained-glass door with this inscription:

BILLIARDS
E.J. REID PROP.

E.J. (Nugget) Reid's three-table pool hall went out of business about a quarter of a century ago, just before the Goolagongs came to town, so I never knew the glories of shooting pool. The Tubb brothers replaced cues with cutlets and eight balls with T-bones, but they didn't replace the door with Reid's name on it. Why should they? The colored glass was pretty and rather posh for a meat market. Besides everybody knew the butchers had taken over. There aren't any secrets in Barellan.

Moreover, the distinctive doorway gives the place an aura it should have, for this is Barellan's shrine. Hanging on a shabby green wall (above the "No Dogs Allowed" sign) is the prized exhibit: a huge fading photograph of Barellan's Greatest Moment, captioned "January 2, 1932, Wheat Carting. 116 Teams, over 600 horses, 13,000 Bags Delivered in One Day, an Australasian Record."

"What a day that was!" beams whiskery Chris Campbell, at eighty-three, Barellan's oldest resident. "Horses and wagons as far as you could see. A man climbed up on the railroad semaphore to take that picture."

It is a picture of horses and mammoth wagons and bags of wheat lined up from those towering silos where I once played at pigeon grabbing high above the town.

"Barellan," says Barry Tubb emphatically, "will never have another day like that." Not even, you gather, if Evonne Goolagong completes a Grand Slam of the Big Four titles in one year by winning at Forest Hills. "That's the last of its kind. Town was lively then but it's going down. Cities are taking over. Young people won't stay, nobody's moving in."

Chris Campbell says, "Our golden age was 1916—just after the railroad come in—to 1952. We had two pubs, two stores, about a thousand people. Lucky to have half that now. Wheat lumping was a profession that's disappeared. Lumpers stacked the wheat. Now machines do it. That big day in the picture, 1932, there was wheat everywhere. Too much for the silos, and they hold 300,000 bushels. Now we've got the Bulkhead, that tin building that holds a million and a quarter. No problems about it sitting in the open once you've brought it to town.

"You worry about that wheat. Will the hail get it? Or the rust? It's a gamble. It's not ours until it's in the silos."

For these cockies (the men who raise wheat and sheep), it's a life of constant toil. They have their prosperous years, but there are years when nature saves too many match points and sometimes steals the match. George Willmer will show you his 2,100 acres of wheat, turning green to gold, as proudly as a nobleman guiding you about his handsomely landscaped estate, and Chris Campbell will recite a few verses of Dorothy McKeller's "My Country": "I love the sunburnt country/ The land of rolling plains . . ."

The plains of Barellan don't roll much. There's a dip here and there, but generally it is as flat as Holland, although way off you can see the hills, Binya, Buryalong, Narriah.

The cockies love their land more than they can say. Summer paints the town red with dust, but rains transform the dust into mud and the fields into emerald, tinged by the purple of Patterson's Curse, the beautiful-but-damned weed that chokes off grass and isn't palatable to the sheep. Rain is good, but too much means rust. It also means wet sheep, the curse of the shearers like my father because, for some reason, the shearer is sometimes overcome by a sensation like the bends in working a damp animal. Too little of course means drought. They can quote you the years of the rains and droughts like a Frenchman reciting vintage years of wines.

Nugget Reid, the ex-poolroom proprietor, won't sell his photo of the Wheat Carting of 1932. Nor will he even give permission for a copy to be made, much to the disappointment of Harry Grant, self-styled town historian. Mr. Reid intends for that holy picture to remain in the butcher shop shrine forever, the property of the citizens of Barellan, or those who make the long pilgrimage to Barry Tubb's for a viewing.

Possibly there's no religion as powerful as the wheat-and-sheep faith of Barellan. They cheer me on the telly from Wimbledon, and I know they're proud of me, but "Will Evonne improve her second serve?" isn't quite as gripping a question as "Will the rust get the wheat?"

Maybe I was Greatest Moment No. 2 when I stormed Wimbledon in Barellan's name. But I can't be sure until Barry puts my picture up in the same room with the pork chops and the Wheat Carting of 1932.

My goal was to win tournaments the first season overseas in 1970. But I had to gain experience against world-class players in all conditions and not to let down those people of Barellan. The second was more important.

I think the feeling of not letting down the homefolks is strongest in those of us who come from the country towns. Everybody in our hometowns knows us, and frequently, as in my case, the townspeople have contributed financially to make coaching and travel possible. I think all Australians are driven by hometown feeling. It's harder for us to go abroad to play the world circuit because of the distances involved. Therefore it's more expensive, and maybe we feel a more compelling obligation to do well. Another factor is our small population. Since there are only 13 million Australians, those of us who come away feel we're being watched by an entire population and that we're really representing our country.

This feeling deepens when we're selected for national teams; for women, the Federation and Bell Cup teams. I'm more nervous for those matches than for anything that happens at Forest Hills. I feel the entire country is depending on me, although, to be realistic, a good portion of my fellow citizens may not be aware these matches are going on. It may not ruin their sleep or their digestion if Australia doesn't beat America to win the Bell Cup or emerge with the Federation Cup from that worldwide team competition.

My first Centre Court appearance in 1970, however, did give me the all-time shakies. Everybody who makes a name internationally in tennis has to undergo a trauma called "Centre Court nerves." You're sure you're going to disgrace yourself, play like a cow, lose miserably, embarrass your friends, and convince the referee that he was a bloody fool to put you on Centre in the first place, a mistake he'll never make again.

Centre Court is the cathedral of the game, and you're afraid you're going to act like a blasphemer. Talk to any of the players who have won Wimbledon. Rod Laver will tell you it's like walking the "last mile" to the electric chair the first time you go in there.

"Centre Court?" I gasped when Mr. Edwards came back from referee Captain Mike Gibson's office. "Why? Why me? For a second-round match?"

Mr. Edwards smiled, "Sweet, you have to play there sooner or later. Might as well get a little used to it. That's where you'll be playing a good share of your matches in future—all the finals."

Jane Bartkowicz, much better known as Peaches, was my opponent, a husky woman with a fierce scowl and a two-fisted backhand who ranked No. 6 in the U.S. Waiting to go on was awful. They put you in a plain room with wicker furniture just off Centre, and you sit there twiddling your thumbs, waiting like a one-legged gladiator who's got to try to outrun a tiger.

Then we were on. I don't remember anything about it, a 6–4, 6–0 beating. No, that's not right. I do recall looking up once and . . . oh, heavens . . . all those faces. Fourteen thousand people! About twenty-eight times the population of Barellan. You could fit the inhabitants of my town into a corner of the standing-room sector and they wouldn't be noticed.

I only looked up once. From then on I kept my eyes on the ground. Occasionally I looked at the ball, but I just wanted it to end as soon as possible, like a visit to the dentist. I wasn't concerned about not letting anybody down. I just wanted out. When we changed ends of the court, I kept walking, never stopping to so much as touch a towel to my brow. If I perspired at all, it was a cold sweat. I wasn't getting enough balls back to work up a sweat. My backhand, usually my most reliable stroke, stood up like butter in the sun.

I wanted out and Peaches let me out quickly enough—mercifully. That wasn't the end of the ordeal. There were still the reporters and the same old questions. As I've said, I have a good relationship with the regulars of the British tennis press. Wimbledon is an entirely different matter. Reporters from all over the world appear, and many are writers and columnists who may never write about tennis except during this fortnight.

What was it like, they wanted to know, to be the first Aborigine at Wimbledon, on Centre Court, playing tennis at a high level? Was my color a problem? Had I been discriminated against? How did I relate to Arthur Ashe?

More race. Always race. Couldn't I be treated merely as a promising young Australian tennis player? Apparently not. I just had to steel myself to the fact that I was different in the eyes of the world, and to try to answer politely when I could, or to say, "I don't want to discuss that, thank you," when I'd had enough. Why should reporters be interested in an eighteen year old who had lost a second-round match to an unseeded and not overly prominent American? That tells you about the world's preoccupation with skin color, doesn't it?

Once in a while someone will say to me, making small talk, "You tennis players sure do get nice tans."

And I'll say, "I've had mine all my life."

Whereupon they reply, "Really? Why . . . oh, I'm sorry, I didn't mean . . ."

So I have to say, "That's quite all right. You didn't say anything wrong. I was just having some fun."

Color is something we joked about with our friends and neighbors at home. But I get tired of hearing about it from reporters, and sometimes I have to tell them. In 1970 Mr. Edwards stayed close by when I talked to the press and let them know when they'd been at me enough. He helped me in those days, and I wanted help. But he's not a ventriloquist. I handle my own interviews and press conferences, and I find myself enjoying them more as I gain confidence in these situations.

You would have thought I was the first Aborigine to discover London that spring and summer of 1970, the way the press swarmed over me. I wonder if they made such a fuss over the Aboriginal sportsmen who actually were the first of my race to compete in England. A cricket team called the Aborigines preceded me to London by 102 years. Brought to England in 1868 by an Englishman named Charles Lawrence, the Aborigines, members of the now extinct Werrumbrook tribe, won half the games on their tour. Their line-up alone should have sold a few tickets, what with names like Sundown, Red Cap, Tiger, Mosquito, Two Penny, Bullocky, and King Cole. Besides, when they appeared the Aborigines offered more than just cricket. They cracked stockwhips, threw spears and boomerangs. That's a tough act to follow.

Well before the cricketers or me there was Bennelong, a full-blooded Aborigine shipped to London in 1792 by Governor Philip of Australia. Bennelong created quite a stir—the black man from the South Seas who was presented at court to George III. He learned English and was a liaison between his people and the English colonizers. Returning to Australia, he lived in a mud hut beside Sydney Harbor on what is now called Bennelong Point. Where Bennelong's dwelling once stood now rises the incredible Sydney Opera House, architect Jöern Utzon's fantasy of giant sails and seashells that became reality and at last opened in 1973 after years of controversy and inactivity.

The career of Lionel Rose, the prizefighter, parallels mine somewhat in that he came in from the country to live with city whites (the family of his manager, Jack Rennie), also won a world title at nineteen, and was then decorated with a M.B.E. (Member of the British Empire) by the Queen. Lionel, who has retired, held the bantamweight championship from February 1968 to August 1969. I used to watch him fight on television, not enjoying boxing but curious about another Aborigine. Mr. Edwards tried to point out the skills involved, but I wasn't interested. "See, honey, when he loses his concentration and drops his hands, Lionel gets a punch in the face." The penalty for lapses in concentration in tennis isn't as severe, but sometimes I think Mr. Edwards wishes it were. That might be one way to shake me up: a jab in the nose.

If my people employed an American press agent, I suppose he'd create an Aborigine Hall of Fame—"a great little tourist attraction, folks." Not likely, of course, but you could get together an interesting collection: Albert Namatjira and Yirawala, painters; Kath Walker, poet; Senator Neville Bonner, first Aboriginal member of Parliament; Dave Sands, Ron Richards, Tony Mundine, Dick Turpin, Lionel Rose, boxers; Harold Blair, singer; Sir Douglas Nicholls, Australian Rules footballer and clergyman; Robert Tudawalla and Ngarla Kunmoth, actors; Harry Penrith, founder of an orphanage akin to Boys Town; Captain Reg Saunders, soldier; Eric Simms and Clive (The Little Master) Churchill, rugby league players; Charlie Perkins, politician and deputy minister of the Department of Aboriginal Affairs; Eddie Gilbert and Keith Dollery, cricketers; "Derby" McCarthy, jockey; Charlie Samuels and Arthur Postle, sprinters. There are others, I'm sure, who would belong. They amount to only a handful, yet considering the obstacles—lack of education, the persecution that is letting up but hasn't faded altogether—my race has included some remarkable people who've made their mark on white society.

Most of them I've named got to London, as I did, at one time or another and ran the gauntlet of questioning reporters, as I did.

Kath Walker, the militant poet, would have had answers different from mine. A spokeswoman for black power, bright and articulate, her experience and outlook are unlike mine. She's politically oriented and motivated. Unless someone speaks out harshly and eloquently, nothing will be changed or accomplished. But that's not my way. I swing a tennis racket and hope my victories can do some good, too, but I'd be dishonest if I said that's why I play. I've gone through that: I play because I love the game; it seems to be what I must do. But if my doing benefits Aborigines in some way, I'm pleased.

There wasn't much relationship between the Goolagong of Centre Court 1970 and the Goolagong of Centre Court 1971. The difference was experience and confidence. I relished returning to Wimbledon the second year, and there would be no more fear of Centre, keeping my eyes on the ground, wishing it would swallow me up. A few weeks before I'd won my first major title, the French Open, proving to myself that I could win in any company, and on slow European clay.

Even if Margaret Court was able to reach out and intercept me on the way to the title, I was now enjoying myself thoroughly on Centre, able to look up at all the people, be warmed by their presence, and even pick out my friends in the multitude.

Losing out on those two break points in the eighth game wasn't going to discourage a Margaret Court. She'd just come at me more determined than ever. Her serve was streaking for the corners in the next game, and I didn't have much play, winning only a point as she trimmed my lead to 5–4. We walked slowly to the umpire's chair to wipe away the sweat and take a sip of juice. Suzanne Lenglen is supposed to have nipped at brandy between games to bolster herself. Brandy would have put me right to sleep.

No time for sleep. Not even for me. Margaret and I were keenly aware of the importance of the tenth game: one set for me, or total recovery at 5–5 for her.

Recovery was the theme. We split the first four points to 30–30. Then I pushed a volley into the net and was enmeshed in another break point at 30–40. Margaret drove a ball down the line to my left, only to be passed as I hit out with a backhand along the same sideline. This confirmed the feeling I'd had all through the match: I could do no wrong with my backhand; it was coming through for me as though I were swinging a magic wand, and I was going to go for my shots on that side until the magic ran out.

Deuce. She sliced a return low and I tried to make a half-volley. Net got in the way. Break point again at her advantage. I slammed my serve for her body again, but she moved neatly away, giving herself room to swat a backhand down the line, a good one. In serving to the left court, I had been leaning that way, and I leaped to my right for the volley, catching the ball firmly on the strings. It felt all right, but there wasn't enough punch in it. No, it wasn't going to clear the net. Right into the tape. That should have been that. However, once in a great while it's the best thing you could hope for, if you've got a nasty turn of mind—a ball that climbs instead of clearing the net. Nobody knows why. Sometimes topspin will give a seemingly losing stroke the boost it needs to hurdle the tape. But this was a volley, hit flat. It climbed anyway, up my side of the white ribbon at the top of the net, to fall exhausted on her side. No play possible for Margaret. She eyed the ball as though it was a rat. Deuce again.

Once more the serve and forehand volley, and this one was clean and hard and darted away from Margaret's hopeless lunge.

That gave me advantage and a game point—set point to be exact. Time to crack down if I could. The crackdown came with an overhead smash. Margaret raised a lob during the rally. I looked up, along with 14,000 interested bystanders, and there against the sky was this tiny white blob. Wait . . . get the racket back and cocked . . . bang! The blob that had been idling above was now lying quietly at the rear of the court where I'd knocked it. One set for me. Six games to four. Mrs. Edwards was pounding Mr. Edwards's shoulder. Barry Court yelled, "All right, Marg, come on now!" but I doubt she could hear him through the applause.

I was halfway there.

A lot of sense and nonsense has been spoken and written about sport bringing together the people of the world. There is a definite value in male and female athletes meeting their counterparts from other countries, in visiting and experiencing different countries and cultures. But these values can be warped and twisted, as in the tragic 1972 Olympics. Athletes are sometimes used as political tools, and sport can become overly nationalistic.

Ideally sport and politics wouldn't be mixed, but this is practically impossible. Near the end of 1970 I was caught up in a very political controversy when I was invited to play in the 1971 South African Open at Johannesburg and accepted the invitation. This, of course, is the tournament that Arthur Ashe sought to integrate in 1969, and for which he was turned down through the South African government's refusal to issue him a visa.

The first nonwhite to win any South African championship was me—the doubles in 1971 with Margaret Court. In 1972 I won the singles, and in 1973 the mixed doubles, with the German Jurgen Fassbender. So I have all three titles, and I think Arthur Ashe will keep trying to win the other two. The singles, particularly, will mean a lot to him and to the South African blacks who were praying for him to come through in the 1973 final against Jimmy Connors.

I've always thought of tennis players as an international sisterhood and brotherhood, people from six continents and many countries who get along together regardless of the ideologies of our governments. Cliff Drysdale, the South African, calls Yugoslav Nikola Pilic a communist, and Pilic retorts by calling Drysdale a racist. That's a conversational opener for them. A Jew from the Netherlands, Tom Okker, is friendly with an Arab from Egypt, Ismail El Shafei. A Russian, Olga Morozova, can communicate with a Rhodesian, Pat Pretorius. And we can joke, too. It happens in other sports, also, and all this is to the good. When Arthur Ashe and Stan Smith made a State Department tour of Africa in 1970, they stopped in Tanzania—a country not especially fond of the U.S.—and were instructed to be prepared for a hostile reception from university students. Tanzanians had been unfriendly to touring Astronauts, so how would they respond to a couple of tennis players in warm-up suits monogrammed U.S.A.?

They responded enthusiastically, causing Ashe to remark, "I guess sometimes athletes can go into areas where others might be rebuffed. We may make small inroads through sport."

Tennis players feel they can go anywhere. I've played every continent but South America and Antarctica, and I'm sure I'll get to those places, too: Antarctica when the construction explosion in indoor courts reaches the South Pole. But we learned in 1969 that there were restrictions on some of us when the South African government excluded Ashe.

By 1971 there seemed to be a slight, very slight, change of official attitude. South Africa itself was being barred and excluded from international sport, and this hit South Africans where they live: on the playground. They're as crazy about sport as we Australians, and they were beginning to feel frustrated by the various boycotts that were started by an English university student, Peter Hain. Hain organized the protest movement that forced cancellation of the traditional tour of England by the South African cricket side in 1971. The argument for the boycott was that apartheid prevented nonwhites from ever being eligible to play on national teams for South Africa. International sport was thus limited to whites. This is obviously wrong, and those favoring a boycott demanded that competition cease between England and South Africa until conditions were changed and nonwhites given a chance.

Those opposing the boycott lamented the mixing of politics and sport, arguing that one country had no right to dictate the sporting policies of another. Why ruin the enjoyment of millions, in both countries, who anticipated these cricket tests with great pleasure and followed them closely?

The boycotters asked: How can you enjoy sport tinged by apartheid?

The boycott was a success. South Africa and England severed

cricket relations. Then the boycott spread to rugby and soccer, also favorites of South Africans. Australia and New Zealand, which also play cricket and rugby, joined the boycotters. Shortly South Africa was thrown out of the Olympics and Davis Cup. South African sportsmen were being shoved further into a corner, deprived of a cherished relationship with the rest of the world. (It's ironic that when the gentlemen who run the International Lawn Tennis Federation evicted South Africa from the Davis Cup, they neglected to make the Federation Cup off-limits as well. This underlined the lack of regard for women's tennis by the all-male ILTF. Under pressure, they banned South African men from Davis Cup play, but nobody mentioned women's competition. Apparently women were below banning, and South African women continued to compete annually in Federation Cup. That's why Russia does not take part and why New Zealand withdrew as host for the 1974 Federation Cup.)

It was questionable whether a sports boycott could make the hard-line South African government waver, despite the discomfort of a sports-mad citizenry. "You can't change them with boycotts," some people said. "Besides, boycotts won't work. Economic sanctions never hurt them."

Remarkably, the sports boycott has worked. As Ashe said in Johannesburg, when he finally got in, "If a country refuses to sell something to South Africa, another country will step in and sell those things and profit. But if a country refuses to play games with South Africa, then it gets serious. Other countries might not play the same games. When you're out of cricket, rugby, soccer, the Olympics, and Davis Cup, there's no place you can look to for the competition you want and need. A sports boycott hurts, an economic boycott doesn't."

When do you lift the boycott? Never, some say—including many nonwhite South Africans—until the government is forced to make substantial concessions in loosening apartheid.

There is some loosening in the area of sport now, but it's hard to tell if it's genuine or just window dressing. I do know that the new South African minister of sport, Piet Koornhof, seems dedicated to bringing his country back into the sporting world. You hear people say in Johannesburg, "If Koornhof can get us back into the Olympics, he'll become prime minister."

Dawie de Villiers, a member of Parliament who once represented South Africa internationally in rugby, has urged that a "way be found so that blacks and whites can play for South African teams overseas." His thought was stamped "logical" by the ultraconservative Afrikaans newspaper, *Die Transvaaler*, which tells you there is a rumbling, however soft, even among those who firmly support apartheid. There has recently been some mixing of whites and nonwhites in track and field, rugby, cricket, and tennis. But is this just show to diminish boycott pressures and disapproval from abroad?

I was the guinea pig in 1971. Owen Williams, the bright, resourceful promoter of the South African Open, worked quietly and carefully at cabinet level within the government to secure an official invitation for me to come to Johannesburg. The invitation meant a visa would be forthcoming if I applied. Owen was fully backed by the South African Lawn Tennis Union, which had earlier lobbied for the admission of Ashe.

The SALTU keenly felt their players' exclusion from Davis Cup and an increase in protest demonstrations against the players themselves when they appeared as individuals in tournaments overseas. At the U.S. Pro Championships of 1971 in Boston, a delegation from the National Association for the Advancement of Colored People picketed the Longwood Cricket Club demanding that South Africans Frew McMillan, Cliff Drysdale, and Rob Maud be scratched from the tournament. Jack E. Robinson, head of the Boston NAACP, said, "If Arthur Ashe is prevented from following his profession in South Africa, why should we let these South Africans earn prize money here?" Robinson and his delegation did more than merely picket. They purchased tickets and sat in the grandstand making the evening miserable for McMillan and Maud by loudly heckling those two throughout their matches. It was a very nontennis scene—incessant noise and insult. Neither player had ever gone through such a barrage while playing, and both were shaken and played badly. The demonstrations, which brought out a very negative reaction from the rest of the crowd, were discontinued, and Drysdale was spared.

Certainly it was in SALTU's and Owen Williams's interest to get the world off the back of South African tennis. I also believe that Williams, Alf Chalmers, and Blen Franklin of SALTU are liberal-minded and would like to achieve genuine integration of tennis in cooperation with the nonwhite tennis federations of that country.

I'd heard from other players what a good, well-run, and tremendously well-attended tournament the South African is, and I supposed —maybe naively—that I'd play there one day. It didn't matter when. I was leaving the schedule, as always, up to Mr. Edwards.

South Africa was just the name of a country and a tournament. I couldn't believe the furor that erupted in Australia when it was announced that I'd been invited to visit that country and play in that tournament. I'd heard of apartheid, but I guess I didn't realize at first how historic my entry into the tournament would be. I had supposed nonwhites could play tennis in South Africa, which they can and do; I had also thought the best could rise to the top as I had in the white sphere of Australian tennis, which they cannot. I learned that the best aren't given the same opportunities as the whites and that they have been barred from the tournaments necessary for improvement.

I would be the first nonwhite, if I accepted the invitation. Would I accept? That's what the press at home and around the world were asking. Besides asking, they already had the answer—their suggested answer: no.

Aboriginal leaders said the same thing—that it would be a slap in the face of my people if I dignified a racist country with my presence and entertained whites with my tennis.

I was the uncomfortable subject of a national debate. I was confused, troubled, and even a little frightened by it all. Mr. Edwards was not. He decided that despite the fuss we would go. "The South African Open," he told the press, "is one of the six most consequential national championships in the world, and it is time for Evonne to play the major titles. We've been assured that she will be treated well—the same as any other player—and I will tell you candidly that if we receive anything less than first-class treatment, or she is subjected to any form of discrimination, we'll be on the first plane out of there."

A story later circulated that I was to be classified as an "honorary white" so that I could go or stay anywhere. That was false. Any nonwhite who receives a visa to visit South Africa on business may live in the best hotels and eat in the best restaurants. During my first visit in 1971 we lived with the parents of Bob Hewitt's wife, Delaille. Since then I've stayed at hotels in Johannesburg, and there've been no problems at all. But it's only because I am an athlete that I don't have to face the indignities that a nonwhite South African must live with.

Margaret Court beat me in the South African singles final in 1971, then joined me in winning the doubles championship. We had departed from Sydney without telling anyone when we were leaving. There was talk of holding antiapartheid demonstrations at the airport, and Mr. Edwards hoped to avoid a trying scene. I can't say whether we would have been demonstrated against, but leaving with no fanfare insured us against turmoil. When we returned, I received a cable from Australian Prime Minister William McMahon, congratulating me on being a "good ambassadress" for all peoples of Australia. We felt we'd done the right thing in going, and Mr. McMahon's message helped confirm our feeling.

We returned to Johannesburg in 1972, both for the Federation Cup and the Open, which I won over Virginia Wade in the final, 4–6, 6–3, 6–0. Although I beat Virginia in my singles to stay unbeaten in Federation Cup for Australia, Britain knocked us out in the semis, 2–1, as Virginia and Joyce Williams defeated me and Helen Gourlay.

Again in 1973 I was back in Johannesburg, and again I was in the final of the South African Open, losing to my rival, Chris Evert. Since her boyfriend, Jimmy Connors, won the singles over Arthur Ashe, the two of them took nearly $30,000 out of Johannesburg in prize money and bonuses in the Commercial Union Grand Prix series. She finished first in the Grand Prix (just ahead of me) among the women, and he finished fourth among the men. That may have convinced Chrissie and Jimmy that two could live as cheaply as one maharajah, whereupon they immediately announced their engagement. Besides they have two-handed backhands in common.

The 1973 South African Open may have been their most significant in that Arthur Ashe finally got in. He had been "too political" before, his 1968 remark, "They ought to drop an H-bomb on Johannesburg," not quite endearing him to the government.

I got into South Africa first surely because I was considered a "safe" import. They weren't certain about Arthur. But Owen Williams, once again maneuvering discreetly in government circles and dealing secretly with Ashe and his agent, Donald Dell, was able to offer the hope of a visa. It was a trade-off. Ashe, older and more diplomatic than in the days of the H-bomb statement, agreed to make no caustic remarks about South Africa before entering or while in the country. "I gain something, and they gain something," Arthur said. "I get to see the country firsthand, so that my remarks later have greater credence, and they get to look a little fairer in the world's eyes by inviting me in."

In 1972 another American black, Bonnie Logan, was admitted to play in the South African Open, as was a French black from New Caledonia, Wanaro N'Godrella. More importantly, a black South African, Dan Beuke, was permitted to enter his homeland's national championship. That was progress of a sort. These three players, however, didn't have the ability or stature of an Ashe, nor the reputation as an enemy of South Africa. Arthur's coming was big news.

"I've seldom been so nervous," said Ashe before he entered the stadium court for his first-round match against a fellow American, Sherwood Stewart. They walked beneath a sign: "Time to Serve Black and White." Was it an omen? No, just a billboard advertising whiskey. Arthur played amazingly well, considering the peculiar pressure of this tournament and the fact that he never rested. He was on the move, talking to as many people of all shades of skin and opinion as he could, trying to learn a maximum about the country and system in a space of twelve days. Arthur was enthusiastically received. Crowds soared to a record 93,000 for the fortnight, even though the main stadium holds only 6,200. Cheers for Ashe from the nonwhite section of the stadium, a small triangular slice of the south grandstand, were loud and appreciative, and Arthur always waved to "my people."

"Arthur does much for our adult morale and to inspire our young players," said Simon Mogotsi, an official of one of the nonwhite federations. "We're praying for him to win."

But he couldn't. Connors was too hot for him in the final. It didn't take Arthur long to become acclimated to the altitude (about 6,000 feet), but he continued to suck oxygen from a portable tank he brought with him to the matches. One white spectator muttered, "I know Ashe doesn't trust us—but did he have to bring his own air?"

Arthur was ambitious to see everything possible. Each time I travel, I try to see more. Travel is broadening, they say, but there are limits for the athlete in making contact with other lands. We're fortunate in getting to so many countries, but like other athletes, most of the time we are in a privileged, rarefied atmosphere. We get the best treatment, meet the more affluent citizens. We can be ambassadors of a sort, but to be realistic, travel for us tennis players is too often no broader than the airport, the hotel, and the courts.

With the South African controversy of 1971 behind us, we headed off to England again as we had the year before to start with the smaller spring tournaments. This time we were adding the French Open to the schedule. Paris in the spring, chestnuts in blossom, the Stade Roland Garros in the Bois de Boulogne—and a lot of Europeans you seldom hear of who know how to play on the native clay very well.

I was beginning to understand more about the game myself. When I started off with Mr. Edwards, I was pretty much a baseline player. I poked my backhand in front of my body, a stroke Mr. Edwards derided as my "Barellan chop." When I was fourteen, it took me a month to get the idea of the backhand, and the stroke was right from then on. I was able to roll it with topspin, slice it, or hit it flat.

For a long while, I had no faith in my volleying, but it came to me after a lot of work. It became second nature, and I was able to rely on volleying more and more. In 1970 I didn't attack too often, but I found myself anxious to get to the net in 1971. I was playing more all-court tennis by then and learning how to win on slow courts like those in Paris. My forehand wasn't as strong as my backhand, but I was hitting it with more power in 1972, and I expect it will keep coming. My first serve got more reliable, but my second still needs work. Nobody explains that to me so clearly—without saying a word —as Billie Jean King and Margaret Court, who attack my second ball and put me on the defensive even though I'm serving.

Although I was seeded No. 3 in Paris, I expected nothing more than high-grade experience in my first major championship in Europe. But I got more out of the trip than a look at the Eiffel Tower and the Mona Lisa. Starting with a South African named Jean Koudelka, I sailed through six rounds without losing a set. Not since Althea Gibson fifteen years before had a woman won the French Open the first time she was entered.

A compatriot from Sydney, Gail Sherriff Chanfreau, did me a favor by knocking off Margaret Court along the way, thus spoiling Margaret's hopes for a second successive Grand Slam.

There's a lot to do in Paris, as you know if you've read the travel pages, but tennis players mainly play tennis. Some see the usual sights, some don't. Chris Evert, making her first appearance in 1973, wanted to know about a great Parisian landmark. "Where's the McDonald's?" she asked her fellow Floridian, Brian Gottfried.

Tom Gorman asked Dick Stockton if he'd roamed through the Louvre. "The Louvre?" said Stockton. "I've been here three times, but I haven't got there yet." Before Gorman could express shock, Stockton continued, "But that's nothing. I went to college for four years in San Antonio and never saw the Alamo."

After beating a fellow Australian, Wendy Gilchrist, and the wily Italian, Lea Pericoli—a woman who endangers birds and low-flying planes with her lobs—I was in the quarters against the local heroine, Françoise Durr. Françoise, in 1967 the first Frenchwoman to win their title since 1948, had become the favorite with Court out of the running.

Self-taught, Frankie came out of Algeria to astound the tennis world with science fiction strokes—strokes so weird that they make the gargoyles on Notre Dame Cathedral seem normal by comparison. She holds the racket as though it were a table knife—but she can cut you up with it. Tremendously accurate and combative, she glares and stomps about the court like Madame Defarge. She twists herself into a pretzel to deliver her backhand, sometimes kneeling in the bargain, but she can put the ball anywhere. Her popcorn-ball serve travels at about four miles per hour, but she places it well and is ready to go anywhere you hit it.

Frankie is a weird experience on court—and a very friendly person away from it. She was showing me plenty I hadn't seen as we split the first six games. French spectators normally pay as much attention to women's tennis as they would to a paté from Wagga Wagga, but we had a good crowd. She and Patrick Proisy were the last of the natives in the tournament, and they were also curious about me.

From 3–3 I guess I completely satisfied their curiosity. It came to me that I could do anything on this clay. Drop shots worked. So did lobs. I was delighted to find that I could come to the net if I prepared my way, zooming up if she gave me a short ball to work with. I served and volleyed now and then, just to catch her off guard. I was driving my groundstrokes to the corners and running happily in chasing down hers. I was learning that I could win points on clay at the net against a sharpshooter like Frankie if I stayed alert and got myself ready to make another volley no matter how good my first volley had been. Australians who grew up as serve-and-volleyers were helpless in Europe until they made themselves realize that their best shots would usually be retrieved and fired back. Once they got over the shock of not winning a point outright with a crushing volley, and tried to anticipate where they'd have to go to make two or three more volleys before the point would end, then they had an idea of how to force and win on clay.

I was in that mood and won nine straight games for a 6–3, 6–0 victory. Nobody had beaten Frankie like that in her own playground.

"You are a magician today, Evonne," she said. "I can do nothing."

Mr. Edwards twisted all those wrinkles of his around into one of the biggest grins I've seen: "That's the best match you've ever played, sweet. The best. You're going to win this thing."

And I did. The semi was another brush with unorthodoxy: Marijke Schaar, a Dutchwoman with no backhand. That sounds wonderful for an opponent, but she has two forehands. Marijke is a sturdy groundstroker who transfers the racket back and forth between hands, depending on where her opponent hits the ball. Of course I assaulted her forehand. There was no place else to go against this ambidextrous and pretty blonde. She gave me a good first set, but couldn't keep up. In 1972 a few connoisseurs of the bizarre eagerly made a pilgrimage to a back court at Wimbledon to watch Schaar against the Indonesian, Lita Liem, in a first-rounder. Liem is also a racket switcher, so there was a match during which not one backhand was struck. The thought must have seemed obscene to referee Captain Gibson, who scheduled it as far out of sight as possible. Liem won the grueling Battle of Forehands Only, 7–5, 7–9, 6–3, and in fact reached the round of sixteen.

I guess Mr. Edwards was a little torn in the final since Helen Gourlay, a Tasmanian who'd beaten Nancy Gunter, had been one of his pupils. Helen is very steady and troublesome. I beat her, 6–3, 7–5, but I had to come from 0–3 and 2–5 in the second set, running out the last five games despite five set points she held against me.

My first major championship at nineteen. Maureen Connolly was eighteen in 1953 when she won in Paris on her first shot.

That triumph seemed enough to make 1971 worthwhile. But Mr. Edwards, regardless of his plans for 1974, was seized by a premonition, and he phoned his wife and said, "Eva, get on a plane. I think you ought to be at Wimbledon."

So we were all at Wimbledon, and everything was apples, as we say in Australia. Actually it was strawberries and cream, in terms of the most publicized item on the Wimbledon menu. I had my music with me, a transistor radio-tape machine that I'd taken to carrying around, and I hoped it wouldn't bother anybody in the changing room. Billie Jean King, the "Old Lady" to many of her colleagues, gave her approval: "About time we had some music in here to liven the place up."

Otis Redding was my favorite that summer, and I listened to a lot of "Sittin' on the dock of the bay." Mr. Edwards can't understand my passion for this kind of music, but he concedes, "It has something to do with keeping her relaxed and happy, no doubt of it."

He likes to tell about a time in Düsseldorf I was playing horribly against the German, Heidi Orth. Lost the first set and was losing the second, whereupon I did a complete turnabout and won rather easily.

"For God's sake, sweet, what was going on out there?" He was a little cross with me. "For the longest time you're playing absolute rubbish, as though you'd forgotten everything you ever learned. Then —like turning on a light switch—everything changes and you become a bloody dream, hitting winners all over the place. Do you mind helping me try to understand?"

"Well, uh, I was trying to think of this tune. It just wouldn't come to me. But there, in the second set, I got it, and started humming it, and everything was all right. Ah yes, I guess I was in a bit of a fog until then."

He gave me one of those "Evonne's round the bend" looks and headed for the bar.

The song was "Ain't No Sunshine When She's Gone" by Bill Withers. Billie Jean may have liked my music, but there was no sunshine for her when she was gone from the semifinals, 6–4, 6–4, on one of my best performances.

I thought I might get a little revenge early in the tournament against Peaches Bartkowicz, who'd gotten rid of me fast, and mercifully, in my Centre Court debut. But she lost to Kristien Kemmer in the first round, and I then beat Kristien. My confidence went up a few notches when I went through Julie Heldman, 6–3, 6–3, and continued to rise when I forgot about a bad first set in beating Lesley Hunt, 1–6,

6–2, 6–1. Arriving in the quarters opposite me was a woman who looks like the Wicked Witch of West Texas when she's gunning those big groundstrokes, Nancy Richey Gunter. Nancy screws in her concentration and turns on a scowl that never leaves. "It scares me to look at pictures of myself playing," she says. "I'm not planning to put an evil spell on anybody; I'm just concentrating, that's all."

She's a grim competitor who has spoken only once on a tennis court. That was in 1969, during a tight three-set Wimbledon match with Karen Krantzcke, who, at 6 feet, 2 inches and 170 pounds, is the biggest woman in tennis. Something went wrong between the two players. Karen thought Nancy was stalling and asked the umpire about it. The silence of a lifetime at the baseline dropped away. "Shut up! You shut up!" Nancy screeched at Karen. "I don't care how big you are—shut up!"

Karen looked as though she'd been shot. Nancy looked as though she wondered who'd spoken. Both are very nice and polite. "I'm sorry, I just want to forget it," said Nancy after she'd won. Tennis can do strange things to people.

Nancy got a 3–1 lead on me in the first set, but I had no intention of staying back and trading punches with her from the baseline. She had me outgunned at that distance. I sliced the ball with my backhand and came in to the net. The slice kept the ball low, and my volleying was working beautifully, so that I could angle the ball and keep her from anchoring herself for the groundies. On a run of five games I had the first set. She took a 2–0 lead in the second, and then I ran six more games for a 6–3, 6–2 win that brought me into the semis against the Old Lady.

Old at thirty? Not Billie Jean. She christened herself "Old Lady" once when she was playing little Rosie Casals. "You're gonna turn me into an old lady if you make me run so much, Rosie," King needled her younger opponent (and doubles partner) at a change game.

"That's O.K., Old Lady," said Rosie, who started the name going public. "I'll still hold you up in the doubles."

Billie Jean King is the most aggressive player I've ever faced. In losing the 1970 Wimbledon final to Margaret Court, 14–12, 11–9—the greatest match I've ever seen—she was fantastic in hitting for winners. They were both superb. Only Margaret could have beaten her that day. Few in the crowd knew that both of them were playing in intense pain with leg injuries. You just won't see a better, more exciting match, a perfect argument against those men who say women shouldn't get equal prize money because we only play best-of-three sets, whereas the men often play best of five. Equal pay for equal work is a male battle cry. Isn't quality more important than quantity?

The brilliance of Margaret and Billie Jean in those two sets exceeded that of most five-set matches.

But this was another year—my year—and in the words of Lance Tingay of the *Daily Telegraph,* "Mrs. King seemed mesmerized by the rapturous quality against her." That was a lovely way to put it.

Billie Jean displayed her customary aggression by rushing the net at every opportunity, and I short-circuited it by belting passing shot after passing shot past her. It was 6–4, 6–4, and I was the youngest finalist since somebody whose maiden name was Billie Jean Moffitt, also nineteen years old, in 1963, also opposing Margaret Court (and losing). For the first time since 1965 the final round would be conducted without the former Miss Moffitt.

Halfway to the Wimbledon championship, with one set in hand, I felt very good. I was convinced I could win, but the essential thing was that Margaret hadn't blasted me off Centre Court. I wasn't letting anybody down. The crowd was with me, and I wanted to keep going and let them know I appreciated their support. But it wasn't all up to me. Margaret had come on strong at the end of the first set after recovering her poise at 0–4. She'd been a little unlucky to miss out on five of six break points, but it was her title I was snatching at, and Mighty Mama wasn't going to hand it away.

You must work hard on that first game of the second set. If you've won the first set you want to keep on showing your opponent you're still in charge. If you've lost the first set, you want to turn yourself around. Very important game, the first one of the second set.

It went to Margaret. In a struggle. She was up 40–15, but made a couple of errors, and I slashed a forehand crosscourt to get a break

140

point. Twice more we went to deuce, and then she focused on my forehand and I bungled a couple of balls.

One-Love for Court. If a fortuneteller had stepped from the grandstand then and said, "Don't worry, dear, Margaret won't win another game," I would have kicked her crystal ball all the way to Piccadilly Circus.

But that's just what happened. Six straight games. I was a little irked at myself for letting the first game slip away after I'd had a break point. I was feeling so free and confident, and I was possessed by such self-assurance that I felt I could outdo her at her own game—serve-and-volley. "Geronimo!" That was my cry. Charge the net every point if at all possible.

I won my serve at 15 to pull even at 1–1. My serve was going fine; volleys were usually my finishing strokes. I jumped on Margaret right away to win three points to 0–40. Maybe I was overeager because she beat me with a lob when I pressed in so close my nose was hanging over the net. That saved one break point. A net-cord volley saved another, her shot just trickling over the tape, and I had no play. But she netted a backhand on the third breaker, and I was ahead 2–1.

Not much breathing room, though, as she forced me to a break point right away. I was attacking on everything, and she was lobbing more, trying to pull me away from the net. Up went a troublesome-looking lob on the break point, and I was trapped. I couldn't have caught up with it if I'd been Phar Lap, the Australian wonder horse. I tried, though, then suddenly relaxed as the ball touched down just beyond the baseline.

From deuce I sprang out of the game to 3–1 with a heavy serve she barely touched, and another serve to set up a winning backhand volley. That opened up some room between us. But if Margaret was to relinquish her championship, she was going to battle as though she was at the Alamo. The last three games were one struggle after another, with the direction of the match seeming to change with every swing of the racket. Break points all over the place for both of us. Deuce after deuce after deuce in a wild bash down the stretch.

Margaret served at 1–3, lost the first two points and won the next three to 40–30. Game point for her. She had so many game points it was hard to keep track of them. But every time she did I whacked a spectacular shot to pull her back to deuce. The first time I knocked her serve right back past her with a backhand. Then I did it again. And then I did the same thing with a forehand. Next I blitzed a lob with an overhead smash: deuce for the fourth time. She got the advantage once more, her fifth game point, but she was justifiably wary of my returns, which had been winging by her like homing pigeons that lived in the corners. When somebody is returning as I was, you try harder to serve well. Too hard, maybe. Double fault. Fifth Deuce. Whack: one more winning backhand return. This was getting monotonous—for her. The sixteenth point of the game became a game point for me—break point.

This is the frustrating, yet marvelous, thing about tennis scoring, the deuce factor, which can make a game like this one a miniwar. She could be within a swing of winning it so many times, and yet with a swing of mine instead—an overhead, murdering a lob—the game went to me.

My hair was matted with sweat, and I kept tugging at it, suspecting it looked awful. But it was no time for the beauty parlor. I needed two more games.

Maybe I was worrying about how I looked for an instant, because I skidded to 15–40, hardly realizing the game had begun. I shook my head and got back to business. Margaret hit a backhand wide to miss out on a break point, and I slugged away a lob to cancel another. My overhead was dynamite. This game was almost a duplicate of the one before. I'd move to advantage for game point, and she'd rip it away from me. Five deuces in this one, too, and one more break point for her. But she never could find the right shot on those crucial points. Once more I wriggled out of the noose, and it was 1–5 as Margaret took the balls to serve for a last time.

Margaret was shaking her head slightly. Then she stared down at her feet for what seemed a long while. It couldn't have been more than a few seconds. She seemed a queen trying to compose herself before walking to the scaffold, hurt and puzzled that her people had turned on her, nevertheless determined to maintain her dignity.

She raised her racket and it must have seemed heavy. Her timing had fled. She couldn't put a ball into the court. The two serves flopped harmlessly into the net for a double fault. She got the next serve in all right, but deposited a forehand into the net. Then a volley. o–40? The umpire said it was true enough: "o–40."

I was going to win. I had thought I could, but now I knew. It was all over. I was absolutely going to win.

While this euphoria was spreading over and through me, Margaret lashed back to brush aside the three match points.

"Deuce," said the umpire, the same man who'd so kindly announced o–40.

Mrs. Edwards gave Mr. Edwards an elbow worthy of a defenseman in the National Hockey League: "Oh, God, Vic, Margaret's going to come back. The child didn't pay attention just when she had it in her hand . . ."

Barry Court was pounding his right fist into his left hand. Mr. Edwards closed his eyes.

But I wasn't walking about. That call of "Deuce!" brought me right back to Centre Court and the threatening person of Margaret Court. She was alive again, and I think she felt if only she could get this game her experience would take her all the way back. You let a person off the hook of three match points and they start getting ideas of winning. Best to squelch that right away. If you can.

Margaret served and came in. I drove my return down the line, and she slid left to make a crosscourt volley. I went down the line again with a backhand, but she intercepted that, too, and poked her volley crosscourt again. A forehand for me, and I intended to give it a good old thrash. As soon as I hit it we both knew the ball was out of sight. She reacted automatically, stretching with a grunt to her left, but the ball flitted through the space between the head of her racket and the netpost and continued straight along the sideline to the corner.

"Advantage Miss Goolagong!" came the call from the towering green umpire's chair. Match point number four. Enough. What was

143

I going to do about it? What was my strategy?

Nothing.

I just crouched and waited for nothing to happen, and it happened twice. The only thing between us was a net of heavy cord, merely three feet high at center. One yard above the ground stood this flimsy barrier, and yet it must have loomed ominously like the Great Wall of China for Margaret. Once she tried to hit a serve over this obstacle. No go, twice.

I'll take it. I'll take a double fault any day on match point, but I don't have to like it. I didn't brood about it. I didn't have any superswat shot in mind to finish off the match with an unforgettable flourish. I was just a touch sorry for Margaret that she finished in a way so painful for a tennis player—the suicidal double fault. It happens. A point is a point. John Newcombe double faulted on match point against Tony Roche in the Forest Hills semis of 1969. Stan Smith double faulted to lose the critical opening match of the 1973 Davis Cup final to Newcombe.

The queen was dead, and there was a new queen: me.

But Margaret didn't pay much mind. She beat me the next time we played, a week later in Dublin.

Around the world people were crying. Trisha, of course, at home in Sydney. Mum at home in Barellan. Mr. and Mrs. Edwards in the grandstand. The people who bet on Margaret everywhere. Barry Court turned around in his seat, kissed Mrs. Edwards and shook hands with Mr. Edwards, and got soaked in the process. "She was too much for Marg today," Barry said. Margaret said the same sort of thing to me. They were very gracious, and that made victory that much sweeter. I didn't want anything to spoil my good relationship with the Courts, but I should have known that a great champion like Margaret can take the few defeats along with the many, many victories.

"Up Barellan!" screamed John Emerson, a neighbor of ours who was watching with my parents. "Up the Moochie!" He and some of the others had called me Moochie when we were kids.

"Thank heaven it's over," said Mum.

Just before the end, Dad took a long swig of beer and hoped "Margaret'll hit these in the net and Evonne will be the champ." He was wishing, but he was right. By this hour it was way past midnight and bedtime in Barellan, but nobody wanted to go to sleep. They all trooped down to the post office on Yapunyah Street, which had been opened especially for the occasion. I told the family I'd phone home after the match, and the only way they could get a call was at the public phone at the post office. There's no phone in our house.

I made the call as soon as possible after the presentation ceremonies, the picture taking, and the interviews. It was probably one of the dullest calls on record. Everybody was so excited they didn't know what to say.

"That you, Mum? Can you hear me? How are you, Mum?"

"Fine, Evonne. Yeah, it's me. Good on you, Evonne."

"Did you see the match?"

"On the telly, dear. Here's your dad."

"Hi, Dad, how are you?"

"How are you, Evonne? It was a beaut match. Do you want to talk to the kids?"

"Ah yes . . ."

"Hi, Evonne, how are you?"

"Fine, Larry, how are you?"

"I'm fine . . . uh . . ."

It went on like that through the entire family and Mr. and Mrs. Kurtzman and some other friends. At a time like that you want to hear the voices from home, the people who were there when you started and have done all they could to help you get ahead.

First prize was $4,320. I had to look that up because I'm never aware of how much I'm playing for. It's incidental, but that doesn't mean I go around lighting dinner candles with ten-dollar bills. I just don't pay attention to figures, which sometimes gets me a scolding from Mr. Edwards.

Most of the time he picks up my checks, but in Tokyo, after an autumn tournament in 1973, he said, "Honey, it's time you started calling in for your money and gathering the checks."

All right. I went to the office, signed for the check, and brought it back to him.

"Did you look at this check?" he was gruff.

"No. Just told them who I was, took it, and signed."

"Well, take a look."

"Righto. $1,200."

"That's right . . . only it's not correct. Don't you realize, sweet, that you won $6,000 for this tournament? This is just a few pennies short. Now take it back and be sure they give you the proper check. This must belong to somebody else."

I couldn't have told you then what the Wimbledon first prize was, but it did mean this to me: I was getting to the stage where the prize money was more than covering my living expenses, and I could start doing some things I had in mind for my folks.

The best present I ever bought anybody, a huge refrigerator, Mum's first, dominates the kitchen. You should have seen her the afternoon the men from the appliance store in Griffith knocked on the door and began carrying in this fridge. I'm sure she enjoyed that more than my winning Wimbledon. And so did I. The sight of her eyes popping was just about the best thing I've gotten out of tennis.

I tried to tidy myself up to meet my first princess—Princess Alexandra—who would be presenting the trophies. Quickly and efficiently, men of the club staff unfolded a green carpet that led from the base of the Royal Box to the net. The ballboys, in their purple and green shirts (the All England Club colors), lined up on either side of the carpet, and the princess proceeded between them to a table on which a Union Jack was folded. There I curtsied before we shook hands, and she handed over the golden platter, the regal symbol in tennis. I had everything a tennis player wants, and I lifted the ornate dish above my head. Princess Margaret and Prime Minister Heath and ex-P.M. Macmillan were clapping. The trophy felt good in my hands, but it was still difficult to realize what it all meant. The battle wasn't far enough behind me. You can't keep the platter. That stays at Wimbledon. Princess Alexandra then handed me the small replica in a leather carrying case that was mine to keep.

We made small talk, but I can't for the life of me remember what we said. It's like a silent movie for the crowd, different from tournaments in America and some other countries. Wimbledon bestows honors quietly. No master of ceremonies, no microphones, no speeches. Mercifully no speeches by tournament officials and tennis association executives.

Sometimes players make choice remarks if they're called on to acknowledge their triumphs. One of the best victory speeches was John Newcombe's after he'd beaten Jan Kodes in a sensational 1973 U.S. Open final at Forest Hills. Newc looked at his check for $25,000 and shrugged. "Fifteen thousand goes to the tax men, $5,000 to my agent and $5,000 to my wife, so . . ."—he threw the check over his shoulder and shook his head. Everybody laughed. Newcombe laughed and decided to pick up the check anyway.

John also starred in his chat with the Duchess of Kent, after she presided at the Wimbledon trophy presentation of 1967.

"What do you plan to do tonight to celebrate, Mr. Newcombe?" wondered the duchess.

"I'm going to get drunk, ma'am," answered the polite and truthful Australian.

I didn't get drunk. There was a rum and coke, which I like occasionally, and some champagne, of course. I'm not a drinker, I'm a dancer. We went to a place called the Knights of Knightsbridge—a disco—to shake and jiggle and gyrate the night away. The music was loud, louder, and loudest. I loved it. Even Mr. Edwards was grinning, the first time he hadn't knocked the rock. If the band had asked him to sit in on bass guitar, he might have done it. "I'll listen to it all night long, sweet," he said. And he did. The headwaiter brought a dish they called "Petite Evonne," which was veal in Madeira wine.

The next night was the Wimbledon ball, customarily opened by the two singles champions. Never before had two citizens of Sydney got it started. John Newcombe and I whirled about to "Waltzing Matilda."

This was another very proud moment for Mr. Edwards because he'd been Newc's first coach. There were his two pupils, displaying their footwork in formal clothing. Newcombe didn't get as much coaching from him as I did, since Mr. Edwards felt "too much formal instruction would make John lose interest." That's what he told Newc's parents. "We'll give him the fundamentals, and then let him go at his own speed." Knowing when not to coach is essential, too.

Wimbledon 1971 had been high season for London's "insulting behaviorists." The pinching of female bottoms may be an exalted male art in Rome, but it's a misdemeanor called "insulting behavior" in London, and you can get arrested for it if a bobby catches you in the act. More than a hundred men were caught and fined during the first week of Wimbledon. Excellent weather seemed to bring out the best in bottoms to the All England Club, to be either saluted or insulted, depending on the custom.

I thought about this when I was called on to speak at the ball. "I still can't believe I've won. Will somebody pinch me? Maybe if I go back to Wimbledon . . ."

Even in Rome I'd have had a difficult time believing it. Winning the final wasn't much different, on first reflection, from winning any other match, really. I didn't say to myself, "You're number one now" or "All my life I've wanted this."

"Can you describe how you feel now?" asked the reporters. "What does it mean to you?" Again I defer to Newcombe, who made the most sensible reply to those questions at Forest Hills in 1973: "Come back and ask me in a month. There's no way to evaluate it so soon after winning. I feel O.K. I don't know what it means to me yet except that I'm glad I won. I won't have to kick myself in the rear for losing." Newc ought to publish a handbook for players entitled "How to Make Acceptance Speeches, Converse with Royalty, and Conduct Press Conferences."

For a couple of hours after I won all I felt was numb. Too many reporters, cameras, autograph hunters, and people wanting to shake my hand. One thing I wanted to do was watch my friend and mixed doubles partner, Kim Warwick, play his semifinal in the men's consolation tournament. We walked to one of the outside courts where he was playing, and—like a bolt of lightning—it hit me: I was Wimbledon champion.

I wanted to scream. Then I felt sick. I thought I might be sick on Kim's court, but I wasn't. What kind of champion behavior would that have been?

Being famous is quite nice at times, and not so nice at others. It's pleasant being recognized, and unpleasant being mobbed.

London is about the only place I have problems. The people are so keen on tennis, and the game gets such broad exposure on television and in the press, that nearly any tennis player is regarded as a celebrity. After I'd become one of the few teen-age champions in Wimbledon history, it was difficult to walk around the All England Club. Crowds converged on me, begging for autographs, and I needed assistance from the police to escape. Bjorn Borg, the pale teen-angel from Sweden who was such a sensation in 1973 and 1974 was the object of even more vociferous affection. Schoolgirls would have torn him apart as an act of love if he'd tried to move about the grounds without a convoy of bobbies.

In the city itself, people are more polite. I'm not regarded as fair game, as I am at Wimbledon. Usually they'll say, "Are you . . . uh . . . Miss Goolagong?" Or I'll hear them whispering. Sometimes I answer, "No, but I guess I do look like her," if I'm in a hurry or don't want to be bothered. Mostly I'll sign for them. I enjoy it, if there isn't a crush.

When Jenifer Edwards is with me she'll address me loudly as "Myrtle" if it looks as though we're going to be surrounded and we're not in the mood. That puts people off.

Being famous complicates relationships with men. If I don't know a man and he asks me for a date, I wonder if he's trying to go out with me or the face in the newspapers. Sometimes it's obvious that he just wants to be seen with Champion Evonne Goolagong and has no interest in me. I say no-thank-you. It's nice when somebody who's never heard of me or doesn't know who I am invites me out. But that can go wrong.

"You mean you're *that* Evonne Goolagong?" he stammers, and then he goes all funny the rest of the evening and can hardly talk. My fame has put the pressure on him.

While fame attracts, it also frightens. A lot of people I'd like to see hesitate to call me because they think I'm too busy for them now. An old friend from the country moved to Sydney but was reluctant to call me for a long time. "I didn't want to intrude in your new life," he said. I scolded him for not letting me know he was in town. People seem to think that becoming famous changes you and that you want to cut all ties with the past. Maybe some people do, but I don't.

The people I wish would call me don't do it enough. I find I have to take the initiative and call them. It's easier that way, I suppose. They never know when I'll be passing through, so when I do I ring them.

That doesn't mean I don't get phone calls from men. I get plenty of them, including a proposal of marriage from an American I barely knew. He called me in Sydney from New York to propose. I told him to keep talking because it must have meant a lot for him to spend all that money—but the answer was still no. I get proposals in the mail, too. I don't answer those.

Few men understand the special demands of my occupation. I have certain obligations that I must see to—my training, my playing, my rest, my tennis-connected business, which includes interviews and appearances. I eat at odd hours during a tournament, and I'm often too tired to go out if I'm playing singles, doubles, and mixed doubles in the same tournament. This puts a lot of men off. My closest male friend, an Englishman, played the tennis circuit for a while. He's sympathetic to my so-called abnormal way of life. We have much in common to talk about. I enjoy his company, but he lives in England, and I don't see him that much.

Right now my commitment is to tennis. The rest will have to fit in wherever possible. I've been reconciled to that from the beginning, giving up the usual social life to get on in tennis, and I don't regret it. There's enough fun, enough parties. Too many parties, in fact, what with all the must-attend functions that are part of the circuit, the receptions where you hear the same question over and over: ". . . and how did you get started playing tennis?"

Another leading question asked of tennis players used to be: "What do you do when you're not playing tennis?" That was in the days when the players were allegedly amateurs and people were curious about how these wanderers supported themselves. Whitney Reed, a legendary American eccentric, would answer, "What do I do for a living, you mean? Oh, I have a paper route."

Impromptu parties with people my age are the ones I enjoy most, where I'm not a celebrity on display. I'm glad I'm old enough so we can have a party on the spur of the moment without putting the guests in a mess the way we did once as juniors in Brisbane. We'd decided to invite some of the boys and girls to my room to listen to music and dance, and the party continued after the hour we were to be in bed.

Mary Hawton, our chaperone, was eventually attracted by the music and rapped on the door. "Get in the bathroom!" we told the boys. "And keep quiet." It was right out of the movies.

"Any boys in here?" asked Mrs. Hawton. "You're up pretty late, girls . . ."

"No boys. We're just listening to music."

"Sounded like dancing . . ."

"Just listening."

"Well, go back to your rooms and get to bed."

Meanwhile, John Alexander, Phil Dent, and the others in hiding were practically drowning. The bathroom was full of dripping tennis dresses that we washed out every night, and the huddled boys were getting drenched for their trouble as dancing partners. They looked as though they were emerging from a rain forest.

At least we can wash our dresses and expect them to dry overnight. It appalls me to think of what it must have been like in that ancient era of B.D.D. (before drip-dry), which wasn't too long ago. Long dresses, petticoats, stockings . . . how did they play, loaded down so?

Elizabeth Ryan, the all-time Wimbledon champion (nineteen titles, all in doubles and mixed doubles between 1914 and 1934), and still a daily communicant at that tournament, told clothing designer Teddy Tinling: "There used to be a drying rack in the ladies' changing room over which we would hang our clothes at the end of a match. Alongside the dresses it was not unusual to see whalebone corsets, stained with blood in places—evidence of the suffering we cheerfully endured in the name of propriety."

Corsets for tennis! If you look at the old pictures, you'll see how ridiculously and uncomfortably swaddled in material they were, dresses right down to the ground. It's a wonder they could move at all, let alone play. When a couple of Californians bared their elbows while winning titles—May Sutton at Wimbledon in 1905 and Hazel Hotchkiss at the U.S. championships in 1909—the spectators were shocked, even disapproving. Sutton (later Mrs. Bundy) rolled up her sleeves to get on with the job, but Hotchkiss (later Mrs. Wightman, donor of the Wightman Cup) appeared in a short-sleeved dress made especially for tennis by her mother.

In our nightly prayers, we female players should have a special word for Billie Tapscott, a South African who liberated the leg in 1929 at Wimbledon by appearing without stockings. She was considered a disgrace by many, and received some vitriolic mail, but Billie's radicalism spread and stockings vanished.

Two years earlier Henry (Bunny) Austin had done the same for the male leg by hacking off his flannel trousers at the knee to create the first tennis shorts. Austin's shameless amputation, and his shins, were subjected to heavy criticism, but you couldn't find a top-class player now who would abandon shorts and play in long trousers.

Teddy Tinling, during four decades of designing tennis costumes for women, has tried hard to bring color, originality, and comfort to his products. He's much more than a dress designer. Teddy's been a friend to the players for years, a striking man of 6 feet, 7 inches whose totally bald head is a beacon above any tennis crowd. He's witty, catty, extremely intelligent, and, most important, a true friend.

In 1948 he blew up his first international sartorial storm by putting colored trim on the hems of the Wightman Cup dresses of Englishwomen Betty Hilton and Joy Gannon. Mrs. Wightman—the same woman who had scandalized Philadelphia with her naked elbows in 1909—objected. "Tennis dresses must be all white," said Mrs. Wightman, although, as she nears ninety, she has accepted the invasion of the courts by pastels and livelier shades. She and Teddy have made up and are good friends.

Teddy's most renowned inspiration was the lace panties he put on American Gussie Moran in 1949. The gentlemen of the All England Club, who have the gall to dictate female as well as male fashion on court, gasped and grumbled at Gussie. Then came gold lamé panties, eighteen carats worth, on Karol Fageros, and an assortment of colors and frills on the underthings of the graceful Maria Bueno.

Rosie Casals is the latest woman whose apparel has run afoul of the stuffed-shirt customs of Wimbledon. Her neat white dress over which flowed a purple floral design was banned in 1972. They told Rosie she'd be banned if she ever wore it again.

Colors are fine, but I prefer basic white with a nice colorful design or trim, like the purple lions' heads along the scalloped hem and the purple buttons on the bodice that Teddy made up for me for 1971 Wimbledon. "Lions for a Leo," he said, referring to my zodiac sign. "You know, my dear, no one can stop a Leo unless the Leo loses interest. Don't lose interest."

I still wear Teddy's dresses in Britain, but I had quite a good contract with Ginori of New York to wear their Goolagong dresses elsewhere. They made them up special for me, but the same dresses went into the retail line. That's unusual, but I think it appeals to women to be able to buy a dress they've seen a top player wearing.

Fame makes endorsements possible. This side of my business is handled principally by Bud Stanner and Jules Rosenthal, executives for International Management, Inc. Mark McCormack launched IMI primarily to help Arnold Palmer capitalize on his appeal as a golfer and currently handles business affairs for about a hundred sportsmen and sportswomen. When Rod Laver sounded out McCormack about taking him on as a client in 1966, McCormack wasn't interested—not enough public interest in tennis. That changed sharply when open tennis arrived in 1968, and Rod was the first tennis player to sign with IMI. Since then John Newcombe, Roger Taylor, Bjorn Borg, Ion Tiriac, Mark Cox, Adriano Panatta, Kerry Melville, Betsy Nagelsen, Manolo Orantes, Laurie Fleming, and I have put our affairs in IMI's hands, along with others such as racing-car driver Jackie Stewart; golfers Gary Player, Tony Jacklin, and Arnold Palmer; basketball's John Havlicek; hockey's Stan Mikita; baseball's Brooks Robinson; skier Jean-Claude Killy; skater Janet Lynn; football's Larry Csonka and Jim Kiick; soccer's Pélé.

Mr. Edwards watches over the endorsements closely so that I don't undertake too much. "The money's good, and it's there," he says, "but the main thing is having enough time for yourself to do what you want, and to get the proper rest you need to play and not feel pushed. If you can't play well, you won't be satisfied, regardless of how much money you make." He's right on that. Losing may not bother me, but giving less than my best does. I don't want to spend too much time posing for commercials or making appearances that will cut into my tennis.

Besides Ginori, I have a worldwide racket contract with Dunlop, and shoe contracts with Dunlop (for wear in Australia and New Zealand) and Romika (for the rest of the world). Part of my off-court financial scheme—along with tennis camps and a position as touring pro for Hilton Head Island, South Carolina—includes endorsements in socks, soft drinks, and cosmetics. These extras amount to something over $250,000 a year. When I think that it's all based on playing a game I've loved since childhood, it's a bit staggering.

I guess I'm well off, but I leave the figures to Mr. Edwards, IMI, and the accountants. The accountants have to wrestle with taxes for every country I play in. For instance, the U.S. Internal Revenue Service takes 30 percent immediately from any prize money; France takes 15 percent; Japan, 20 percent. It's different everywhere. For

154

some countries you file later. Australia takes into consideration the payments I make abroad. I'm glad somebody else is doing the arithmetic. Mr. Edwards says I realize roughly one-third of what I gross, and that doesn't seem bad.

I was wary of the IMI people at first. They seemed like the fast-talking American big-businessmen that you see in the films. Maybe they are, but we've established a nice relationship, and they're very considerate of my time and feelings and just how much and what I'm willing to do.

They're delighted with my fame. Who wouldn't be, when they're taking a percentage of it? But they wouldn't be getting that percentage unless my watchdog, Mr. Edwards, had agreed first. Most pro tennis players have agents now. Mr. Edwards looked over numerous agents before we signed with IMI.

And only a short time ago I thought an agent was somebody who chased crooks for the FBI.

Is it all too much too soon?

I'm not talking about money: money to me means asking Mr. Edwards for $50 or $100—what Sugar Ray Robinson calls "walking-around money." And occasionally Mr. Edwards says, "You've been going a little heavy, lately, honey. It doesn't grow on gum trees, you know." I know.

And I'm not talking about fame. Money and fame just don't turn me on that much. What I mean, and what Mr. Edwards worries about, is competitive success. Did I have too much too quickly when I won the French Open on the first try, Wimbledon on the second in 1971, the South African on the second in 1972, and the Italian Open on the first in 1973?

His timetable was explicit when we set out to travel the world in 1970: "I've got a future world champion here in Evonne. She'll win Wimbledon and be No. 1 by 1974. That's when she'll be reaching the height of her physical and mental powers in tennis."

So 1974 was the year we were pointing for. Anything I accomplished up to then would be gravy. There's been a lot of gravy,

155

particularly those major championships I mentioned, as well as the National Indoor title of the U.S. in 1973—altogether seventeen singles championships of thirteen nations by the start of 1975.

Although 1974 was certainly a very good year, it wasn't the grand success that Mr. Edwards had envisioned. No Wimbledon, no Forest Hills. The start was everything we wanted—my first Australian Open title, over Chris Evert in the final to boot. But there was no hope of a Grand Slam because the French closed the door to us WTTers. Wimbledon was my most disappointing, a fourth-round loss to Kerry Melville in which I threw away countless opportunities. I came into Forest Hills extremely keen, WTT behind me, and I played some of my very best tennis, even though I didn't win. Starting the semifinal against Evert I was just about perfect, running the first set out in six games. I was a game away from victory in the second set when rain stopped us for two days. She returned to the court grimmer than ever and won the second set in a tie-breaker. Here we were, in another of our relentless struggles. Chrissie had won fifty-six straight matches, eleven straight tournaments, but I brought her down, 6–0, 6–7, 6–3. That felt good, and so did a final round triumph over her at Denver a few weeks later.

It looked to just about everyone that I was going to take my first U.S. Open crown when I got ahead of Billie Jean, 3–0, on one service break in the third set of our final. We were both bombing away in a match exciting to play and watch. I just couldn't hold her off. She's unbelievably competitive in a situation like that, the best competitor in the game. Our shotmaking kept the full-house crowd of over 15,000 roaring and applauding, reacting instinctively to both of us. There was no partisan cheering against either one as in WTT. They were just swept along as Billie Jean and I attacked each other. From 0–3 she won five of the next six to 5–4 and served for the match. I resisted, breaking her at love. Suffering in the grandstand, Larry King said to a friend, "What would the odds be against Billie Jean losing her serve in four points when she's serving for a championship? Five hundred to one?" It may have seemed like anybody's match at 5–5, but her will was too much. She won eight of the last nine points. "Never had to work so hard for a title," she said. I said to the press, "I can't understand how you call her the Old Lady, the way she moves."

For female pros, the climax of the year was October, in Los Angeles—the $150,000 Virginia Slims Championship. This was my finest hour: I beat Billy Jean for the second time—the first since Wimbledon 1971—in the semifinals and at last overtook Chrissie in the final, 6–2, 6–3, which meant I was ahead in our rivalry 8–7. The prize money—$32,000—is the biggest purse in women's tennis.

Mr. Edwards questioned whether winning meant as much to me after all that success, and that's a good question. I think it does, but I can't be sure. I'd like to win a Grand Slam. Only Don Budge (1938), Maureen Connolly (1953), Rod Laver (1962 and 1969), and Margaret Court (1970) have made the Slam.

If I don't win another Wimbledon, I'm not going to brood. I'd like to, but . . .

Fitness is almost a religion to Australian sportsmen. More important than talent is being in shape to stay on the court all day, and then some. To get ready for the overseas trips I ran for miles, sprinted and jogged, spent time in the gym (Dupaine's Institute) doing calisthenics and medicine ball reflex training with Jim Craig, skipped rope —500 to 1,000 skips at a time—and worked on my breathing. We'd go to the Edwardses' beach home at Wamberol and run in the sand —that's work! When the training was over we'd go in the surf, which I learned to love, although the first time was a scary experience. I thought the ocean would be just like swimming in the river . . . until I got dumped by a huge wave. Where did that come from? All of a sudden I was spinning and churning as if I were in a washing machine, and swallowing water. For an instant, I thought I'd had it, but I bobbed up and everybody was laughing at me. "Not quite the Murrumbidgee or one of those dams in Barellan, is it?" roared Mr. Edwards.

By the time I get onto the circuit, just practicing and playing is enough to maintain my fitness.

While I was winning Wimbledon, a little girl across the Atlantic Ocean named Christine Marie Evert was getting ready to tear up the

157

U.S. Open at Forest Hills—almost. Billie Jean King stopped her in the semifinals, but not before unseeded and amateur Chrissie had astonished and electrified the American sporting public by coming on like a cavalry rescue after losing the first set and then beating in succession Mary Ann Eisel, Françoise Durr, and Lesley Hunt, all seasoned pros.

Only the 15,000-seat stadium at Forest Hills was big enough for her matches, as this sixteen year old caught the fancy of the press and the customers. After that, the referee wouldn't have dared schedule her anyplace else because the crush of spectators trying to get a glimpse of her would have caused a riot. To this day Chris Evert has rarely played singles at Forest Hills anywhere but the stadium courts.

That's when I began paying attention to Chrissie, although I'd heard of her a year before when—at fifteen!—she beat Margaret Court at a small tournament in North Carolina. Mr. Edwards had decided I wouldn't play Forest Hills, disregarding some clamor from America for the presence of the Wimbledon champion. They didn't need me, what with the rise of Chrissie.

Before she left Forest Hills, to return to high school classes at Fort Lauderdale, Florida, Chrissie mentioned my name. She said she was thinking about that girl on the other side of the world. That girl was thinking about her, too. We wanted to meet and play, and I don't think it was immodest of us to speculate on a relationship that some writers would anticipate as the Rivalry of the Seventies, and feel that we might be the dominant figures in the women's game. We were curious about each other, conscious of our similarities as well as our differences. She grew up in a tennis family (as I had once I moved to Sydney), daughter of teaching pro Jimmy Evert. We both grew up beside the sea, she at Fort Lauderdale and I at Sydney, and there was competition within our families. She had her younger sister Jeannie, who holds a national women's ranking in the U.S., and I had Trisha. Theirs is a Catholic household, as was ours (with the exception of me and Mr. Edwards), and Mr. Evert seems as strict and principled as Mr. Edwards. Neither man is money-driven, although they aren't casual about it either.

158

But Fort Lauderdale isn't Sydney, and the U.S. isn't Australia. I think kids mature a little sooner in America; I've never seen anyone so self-assured as Chrissie, so businesslike and intense in her concentration. If she smiles while she's playing, it's rare. If I don't, check my pulse and send flowers.

Her two-fisted backhand makes her unorthodox—or does it? Because of the Chrissie Craze, every kid in America seems to be swinging in the two-fisted baseball style. "I didn't teach it to her. I wouldn't teach it to anybody," says her dad. "She picked it up because she wasn't strong enough to hit a backhand with one hand when she started. Who am I to change a stroke that is so good and successful?" Jeannie Evert is a double-hander, too. At the age of two, Clare Evert was swinging a flyswatter with both hands, taking it out on insects as she got ready to emulate Chrissie and Jeannie.

Chrissie and I weren't the only ones thinking about each other. Tournament promoters everywhere were anxious to get us together. It was a natural match that would sell tickets. Nancy Jeffett, who operates the Maureen Connolly Brinker International, a winter indoor tourney, thought sure she'd have our series opener when we both accepted invitations to go to Dallas in March of 1972.

We met for the first time at the T-Bar-M Racquet Club for the Connolly and you'd have thought it was a summit conference the way the reporters followed us around, intent on being within earshot when we said the initial hellos to each other. We met socially and liked each other, but we did not meet on a tennis court. Billie Jean King, extremely reluctant—as has been Margaret Court—to cede the 1970s to Chrissie and me, saw to that by beating both of us before, exhausted, she lost the final to Nancy Gunter.

I don't know who made the draw for that tournament, but it sure was crook, which is Australian for sick. Here were Goolagong, King, and Evert—Wimbledon champ, U.S. Open champ and semifinalist—all in the same half of the draw.

If Chrissie feels the way I do, she's glad she didn't play me in Dallas. We had to wait four months to gun away at each other, but it was worth the wait because our shoot-out became a very special occurrence at a very O.K. Corral called Centre Court.

Would I feel it was so special if I'd lost? Yes, because of the tension and suspense beforehand, the excitement of the match itself in which I fell behind, and almost out, and the publicity and attention it got. This was our occasion—it belonged to Chrissie and me—as well as those who sat in on it. She tells me that people continually ask her about that match. Same with me. It doesn't matter who won when you look back. It was the semifinal, and Billie Jean took away my title without much trouble in the following round. But to me and Chrissie, that semifinal was the tournament. We'd pointed for it as soon as the draw was announced and our names popped up in the same half, with me seeded No. 1 and Chrissie No. 4. The rest of the tournament was anticlimactic, if Billie Jean will pardon my saying so.

Winning was better than losing, of course, and that match made the year for me, a year for which I was classified as "disappointing" by most of the critics. I didn't care what the reporters said. I seldom read their stories—although I'll admit that one of them fired me up for a while. Covering the British Hard Courts at Bournemouth, Peter Wilson wrote in the *Mirror*—after my sloppy win over a minor Englishwoman, Alex Cowie—that he'd never seen "such dribble played by a Wimbledon champion." Mr. Edwards put the story in front of me at breakfast and said I might find it interesting.

That afternoon I beat a leading German, Katja Ebbinghaus, 6–0, 6–0, in twenty-nine minutes. I followed that with a 6–0, 6–2 win over Sharon Walsh and a title-round victory over Helga Masthoff, 6–0, 6–4. I guess Peter Wilson's needle got to me.

I wasn't disappointed in myself for the year. After all, I won most of the matches I played and quite a few tournaments, and throughout the year I felt something new: pressure—pressure to live up to what I'd done the previous year at Wimbledon. Suddenly people expected me to win everything.

I wasn't disappointed in myself, but I knew I was disappointing all those people I didn't want to let down. I sensed a slight, but real change in attitude of some of my friends. Hardest to take was the reaction of Mr. Kurtzman, who couldn't seem to understand why I would lose now. Hadn't I become No. 1 in the world in 1971? Wasn't I young and constantly improving? How could anybody beat me? Especially with Margaret Court withdrawn from the circuit to have her first baby.

Mr. Kurtzman wasn't a knocker by any means. Nor were any of the others whose opinions meant something to me. He was gentle in his letters, but there was no mistaking his puzzlement, his wondering if I was doing something wrong, not quite bearing down as much as I should.

"I'm trying as hard as I can, but they don't seem to understand that," I'd say to Mr. Edwards, self-pityingly. "What do they expect?"

"Everything, honey. Everything," he said. "I know you're trying hard. Too hard. You're pressing. This is the difficult year, after you've won your first big championships, and people get the idea that they'll keep coming in automatically now. You and I know it doesn't happen that way. They mean well. They love you and want the best for you. But they haven't been in big tennis as we have. They don't understand what you're going through and how every opponent now points for you, the champ. They're just not close enough to it.

"So you'll just have to be understanding of their concern. And forget it. You've made such a big hit that you can't hope to live up to it all before you're twenty-one. I think you're doing fine. You're ahead of our timetable. As long as I'm satisfied, let's neither of us worry."

The first day of Wimbledon in 1972, I was greeted with: "Good day, Cuddly."

What was that?

"You do look cuddly, you know."

"I beg your pardon . . ."

Several people I knew, all male, called me "Cuddly" that day. What was going on? Had I missed something somewhere?

I had. In my usual neglect of the newspapers, I hadn't seen a drawing of me in the *Sun*—a drawing of all of me in the altogether —by Paul Trevillion. I've never been so embarrassed. There I was in several million newspapers, chasing a ball at full stretch dressed only in a tennis racket. No clothes at all. I was totally flustered. Was the man a Peeping Tom? Where had he ever seen me undressed? Even if he had, how could he put it in the paper? What sort of a newspaper was this? I wanted to go hide.

The caption under the drawing said: ". . . she's soft, round, cuddly like a tennis ball . . ." So that's where all this "Good day, Cuddly" came from. Mr. Edwards had seen it right away, and he was furious. He wanted to strangle the artist, or at least boil the bloke in his own ink.

"What the hell kind of journalistic standards are there that this can go on?" he roared. "Isn't there any right of privacy against something so depraved as this?"

We learned that Trevillion was in the midst of a series called "The Naked Truth of Sport" in which he depicted sportsmen and sportswomen as he imagined them nude. I wasn't the first victim. He'd even drawn Princess Anne, a world-class horsewoman, in the role of Lady Godiva. If he could get away with that in England, I guess there was no reason why he wouldn't try a tennis player. That didn't mean we had to like it. Mr. Edwards inquired into lawsuits, and Dennis Howell, a member of Parliament, brought it up in Parliament, complaining about the "debasement of proper standards of journalism." The *Sun* was eventually rebuked by the British Press Council, but apparently there were no grounds for suit.

I don't know what this artist would have done if he'd known that Barellan is nicknamed Naked Nan at home (in Australian slang Barellan becomes Bare Ellen, thus Naked Nan), but I'm glad he didn't. It was bad enough.

Wimbledon, which had been so joyful for me, became an ordeal. I hated to go to the grounds because I thought everybody knew about the drawing and was imagining me undressed. It made me feel all funny. I wanted to get out and go home to Sydney. It didn't help my tennis. I was really lucky to beat Olga Morozova in the fourth round, 3–6, 6–0, 9–7, after she'd served for the match in the third set, and

Françoise Durr in the quarters, 8–6, 7–5, after she'd served for both sets.

But Chris Evert was up ahead, a challenge that was on my mind, and I didn't want to miss her. Thoughts of that drawing were blotted out by the nervousness of going onto the same court with Chrissie. It was a good nervousness, the kind that always makes me keen, glues together my concentration and helps me to play my best.

Chrissie didn't have it too easy either. Converged on by the press, she was the teen phenomenon I'd been the year before. They built up a nonexistent romance between her and Jimmy Connors, although maybe they became a case of life imitating journalistic art. They became acquainted at that Wimbledon, and though stories of an engagement at the time were preposterous, an engagement was formally announced by the two of them at the end of the following year. "The reporters are all over. They camp on our doorstep," sighed Colette Evert, Chris's mum. By autumn 1974, the engagement was off.

The press can drive you right out of your tree, especially at Wimbledon, because you're not dealing solely with the usual tennis writers. The newspapers assign task forces of reporters to chase down every item. With so many papers in London, each one trying to come up with a different angle, you get an awful lot of pestering. I have great respect for the English tennis writers, but not much for the sensationalizing the papers indulge in during Wimbledon. It's a time when they lean heavily on that old journalistic guideline: don't spoil a good story with the facts.

Chris lost her introductory Wimbledon set to Valerie Ziegenfuss, but won in a struggle. It took her three sets to get rid of Patti Hogan in the quarters. So there we were in the semis after months of anticipation. The build-up was more like that for a heavyweight championship fight. Evonne Sing-a-long against the Ice Maiden . . . the South Sea Princess versus the American Girl Scout . . . Match of the Decade . . .

Teddy Tinling was as jittery as a cat with a hot tin of marijuana going through an airport search line. "Never been anything like it," he said. And he goes back a long, long way. "Great players have met before, but not in these circumstances, not for the first time on Centre Court. It's amazing they haven't played before, but it's marvelous. It heightens the drama. The only thing I can compare it with is 1926, that one time Suzanne Lenglen, the great champion of the 1920s— perhaps the greatest of all—played young Helen Wills, who at twenty was on the way up as Suzanne's successor. That was splendid theater —Suzanne won—but after all it was the final of a minor tournament at a small club in Cannes. Not a setting to be compared with this. Of course Evonne and Chrissie will play many times, unlike Suzanne and Helen, but we'll cherish the first."

Teddy was taking it very personally. "My prestige is on the line . . . I'm a wreck," he wailed. He felt himself to be in a very real competition, too, since I was wearing his designs while Chris was showing off those of Mondessa Swift, an American. Teddy may have a little Aboriginal witch doctor blood in him. He can turn on the most frightening evil eyes this side of Dracula. He fastened them on Bobby Riggs throughout Billie Jean King's victory over Bobby, and he flashed them at Mondessa while Chrissie and I were batting away at each other. He has too much of the gentleman in him to give Chrissie the evil eye, however.

Teddy pointed out another similarity to the Lenglen-Wills confrontation: "Evonne is dashing, gay, and nimble like Suzanne. Chrissie is dour, withdrawn, and mechanical like Helen. But make no mistake about Miss Evert. She may not be as graceful or as much fun to watch, but she's so determined that when she matures she may go years without losing, the way Wills did."

Although they publicized her and read about her and watched her, the English did not wholeheartedly take to Chrissie. "She's such an ice-cold pro that we don't understand her," a friend said to me. (He knew she was actually an amateur, but she acted like an old pro when she played, all right.) "To us a seventeen year old should be a giggly schoolgirl, not a self-assured prima donna of Centre Court. She's so bloody unaffected and ruthless out there . . . she's inhuman."

Well, that's the way Chrissie affects you when she plays: "a well-trained poodle on parade, en route to winning the blue ribbon at a dog show" is the way Dave Anderson described her in the *New York Times*.

Moreover, the English were skeptical of her American successes. The English are skeptical of anything that happens in the Colonies. They didn't quite believe the tales of her staying at the baseline on Forest Hills grass to beat away her attackers with groundstrokes. They couldn't understand how partisan and adoring the American crowds had been. ("It's hard enough fighting Chrissie, but I couldn't fight 14,000 people, too," wept Lesley Hunt, one of her U.S. Open victims, who left the court beaten and crying. "It's an awful experience to have everybody against you.")

Chrissie's appeal was lost on the English. Their curiosity remained high, but once again they were with me on Centre Court. Not so openly as the Americans had been for Chrissie ("They applaud my double faults!" blubbered Françoise Durr at Forest Hills), but I was their girl. It's a nice feeling, but I know it can change one day, when a new darling comes along. Billie Jean discovered that, as have numerous others. Fans pay money, and the privilege to be fickle comes with the ticket.

If we looked cool when we came onto Centre, after Billie Jean had eliminated Rosie Casals in the afternoon's first semi, it was strictly a pose. We were shaking. This was it. I wasn't relaxed the way I'd been against Margaret in the final a year before, knowing I had nothing to lose. Here I had the title to lose, and I was being threatened by another wonderchild.

It wasn't a grudge match, though, and I hope the press never builds our rivalry into that sort of thing. Chrissie and I aren't close, but we've always liked and respected each other. We're linked by our attitudes and our ages: young women who go their own way. We'd stayed aloof from the two women's unions that have sprung up, refusing to ally ourselves with any group or cause. Our money is handled for us and doesn't concern us. We're united by mutual admiration and by a desire to beat each other as badly as we can while we're playing.

165

I enjoy playing her so much. I always know the score, which means I'm concentrating, responding to her challenge. She has said of me, "I feel a good relationship with Evonne. I play hard as anything against Evonne, but I don't really enjoy beating her that much, and I don't mind losing to her. Not like I mind losing to Billie Jean or Margaret. I really savor victories over them. But with Evonne it's just comfortable. Oh, we try hard to beat each other, but it doesn't carry over, somehow. It's a very nice rivalry."

The Very Nice Rivalry began with Chrissie asking me about curtsying to the Royal Box. She was new to this. "Just sort of bend your knees and bob," I said. I never do the very formal curtsy I learned when I made my debut at that Sydney ball with Trisha. That's a bit much. We're here to compete, not to dance and socialize. We bobbed, and giggled, knowing how awkward and silly we appeared. Two fine athletes who looked about as coordinated as the Tin Man when his joints were rusty. The story in the *Boston Globe* said we "resembled a couple of Protestants trying to genuflect at Lourdes."

We recovered control of our bodies quickly enough, and for ninety-five minutes we ran, stretched, lunged, and sprawled. We hammered, smashed, stroked, nursed, blasted, and blooped balls over the net, producing the kind of drawn-out spectacular points that make tennis excruciating for spectators and nearly impossible if the spectators are your people. Mr. Edwards was smoking a pipe this time. Amazingly, he did not bite off the stem or swallow it. Mrs. Evert was chewing gum, madly. Somehow she refrained from breaking her jaw. With Mrs. Evert was Reverend Vincent Kelly, the principal of Chrissie's school. "I just prayed that Chrissie wouldn't be outclassed and overwhelmed. That's all," said Father Kelly. He was fair about it.

No danger of her being overwhelmed. I found out quickly how tough she is from the baseline, on fast grass or slow clay. First point of the afternoon: I drove a backhand down the line and came in to volley. What volley? Her crosscourt forehand went past me so fast that I made a funny, unbelieving face.

Even so, I broke her serve in the opening game, to a murmur of approval from 14,000 voices. But she hit her groundstrokes so firmly that I was rushing my volleys or mishitting them. The first three times I tried to serve-and-volley she whizzed passing shots. I couldn't touch the ball. It made me respectful. I realized I could only come in on the very best approach shots.

She was drilling the ball in a way I'd never seen before. Chrissie isn't stronger than Margaret Court, but she has a different game. She seems to think she'll get a nosebleed if she comes to the net, so she hangs back there like a battleship shelling a port miles away. Boom, boom, boom . . . over and over again . . . harder and harder and harder. I wondered where the power came from. Chrissie was slight and slim (although she's filled out since), but she had balance and timing, a tireless rhythm, and she could think. She was a metronome with a brain, changing speeds, catching me with a beautifully disguised drop shot. She would lure me up, then pass me. I tried to get her to come up, but she wanted no part of it. If she was out of position, she'd sky a good lob, buying time to regroup.

It was marvelous stuff, and before I knew it she'd moved from 1–2 to 5–2. I was serving then and she got the first two points. But I made a couple of winning volleys, and on a run of eight points I'd held my serve and broken hers at love as she served for the set. Now I was 4–5 and feeling confident, with my backhand and swooping volleys functioning well. I was reacting to danger the way I so often do, and I was ready to take over.

Chrissie wasn't ready. She banged away at my backhand, and it went to pieces. Instead of tying it up, I lost serve and the first set, 6–4.

I kept losing. A bit of walkabout here? I don't know, but I was just about out of it at 3–0 for Chrissie. The crowd was as lethargic as I was. At 40–15, with me serving the fourth game of the set, Chrissie got a point on one of the rare bad bounces on that court. I grinned at the bad luck. That revived the audience. I revived, too, and won six straight games for the set.

It was obvious I couldn't beat her from the baseline. I couldn't outboom a battleship. I had to move her around, put her off balance, a little more on the defensive, so I could creep up and do some volleying. At 0–3 it was now . . . or forget it. I started to think about

Mr. Edwards's advice. I never want to hear about strategy before a match. I simply play. But this time, because I was going against the unknown with Chris, I had asked him, "What should I do?"

"You've got to take advantage of her double-handed backhand," he said. He'd coached Jan Lehane O'Neill, a fine Australian who uses both hands for her backhand, and he knew the weaknesses. "Slice your backhand short crosscourt to her backhand. She has to take extra steps to handle anything on the backhand, but if she has to go after a low, short ball, she'll work that much harder. She can't hit it as well on the run, and she doesn't bend too well. Pull her out of position that way."

I thought about it, tried it, and it worked. It's not that easy to do. But when I could hit the low spinning ball I wanted crosscourt, with good angle, it opened up the court for me. When she was hurried like that, she merely put the ball back over the net. She didn't drive it, and I was there to cut off her shot with a volley.

We'd played almost an hour and were even at a set all. I was brimming with confidence, serving hard and well. I felt I knew how to beat her, but it was far from over. I won my serve, a seventh straight game, and the streak ended as she won hers. Those were a couple of routine games, sort of a lull before the storm resumed.

After that every game was hectic. Break points were everywhere, to be escaped and made. She broke me, and I broke her back to 2–2. A mighty forehand return broke me once more, and Chrissie was ahead again at 3–2.

I wouldn't let her hold serve, getting to 3–3 on a leaping forehand volley. My serve. I double faulted to break point, only to wipe it away with a serve that buzzed through her. It was 3–4, and I held a break point that vanished on the strength of one of those ripping double-handers. "Game to Miss Evert. Games are four all, final set," chanted the umpire.

She was weakening, I thought, even though she held serve. She'd butchered a couple of vital overheads and was shaky if she had no alternative but try to volley, when I'd dragged her close to the net.

O.K. Got to hold serve. I was pumping the first serve in and at

30–0 I decided to try a serve-and-volley. She'd passed me every other time, informing me that I'd have to work my way forward, not come steaming in on the serve. This time it worked. Her return wasn't as sure or solid. I knocked it off with a volley and quickly had the game to 5–4.

If she held, it might go on forever. All afternoon she'd been killing me with that cute, deceptive drop shot, halting a big swing abruptly to deliver a wristy flick. She tried it a last time. I had it picked and sprinted ahead as she caressed the ball. It was barely over the net, but I was there to transform it into an even meeker drop that lurched above the net and expired on her side. She nodded almost imperceptibly. Nobody had treated her drop shot that way. Few had ever reached it.

She served and we slapped the ball back and forth. It came to my forehand, and—I don't know why or how—I made up a shot. At least I'd never hit the shot before: a forehand crosscourt chop that sat down almost as soon as it touched the turf. She was waiting with her forehand, but the ball curled back away from her, bouncing only a few inches. Again she had no play: 0–30. I was playing out of my mind, and all the pressure was on her. I sliced again to her backhand, and she knocked it into the net.

Match point. Lots of them.

One more slice to the backhand. Not a very good one. She was there in time to blast a backhand crosscourt. I glided to my left and cut one last angle with a backhand volley. She didn't bother to go after it. Better than anyone she knew it was no use, but she kept coming for her closest look at the net. To shake hands.

Not a great match technically, but everybody called it a sporting epic, and I'll accept that verdict. In winning, 4–6, 6–3, 6–4, I'd come from a set down and 0–3 in the second—and from 2–3 after losing serve in the third. I was more than satisfied.

It was, as I would realize later, something in the bank for the future. Chris beat me the next five times we played, but the recollection that kept me from going up the wall was that first match. I knew I could beat her because I'd done it. I knew that eventually I'd do it again, and I won four of the five that followed. We were even, 8–8 by the end of 1974.

Chrissie cried a little in the changing room, but she didn't lose her sense of humor. When a reporter told her that I'd followed Mr. Edwards's game plan, she remarked, "Oh. Well, I made my own plan, and you see where that got me."

Billie Jean said she'd "waited 365 days to get even with Evonne." She was entitled. She was psyched up to regain the Wimbledon title she hadn't held since 1968. I was the one who kept her out of a sixth straight final in 1971, and she'd been smarting about it since.

That's what makes her one of the greatest players in history. She can get herself worked up to the sky. Ask Bobby Riggs about that if you don't believe me.

I tried. Don't let me take anything away from Billie Jean King's 6–3, 6–3 triumph. She jumped on me for a 4–1 lead, and though I got back to 3–4 with my serve to come, there wasn't much doubt about which way it would go. I just wasn't there, and I don't mean walkabout. For me, The Match had been the semifinal with Chrissie.

How could a Wimbledon final be a letdown? Only in an instance like this, I guess.

When I tried to serve-and-volley out of match point and she whipped a backhand by me, I was actually relieved. I was totally bared at Wimbledon: Trevillion, the artist, had stripped off my clothes; Billie Jean had stripped off my title.

The loss of weight was refreshing. I wasn't the Wimbledon champ any more, and I didn't have to prove anything to anybody for a while. I'd beaten Chrissie, gotten to the final. That was enough. I didn't want any more, although we were committed to go to America for a few tournaments and the Bell Cup prior to Forest Hills.

Indianapolis (National Clay Court Championships), Cincinnati (Western Open), and Cleveland (Bell Cup) I liked. Midwesterners were friendly and hospitable. The atmosphere of the events was pleasant. But New York? I wouldn't want to visit or live there. Noisy, dirty, frightening. I had all the usual complaints. The people seemed

170

rude. The press were all over me as usual, but they seemed more aggressive about it, and they weren't as knowledgeable about tennis.

The West Side Tennis Club at Forest Hills in Queens, venue for the U.S. Open, has none of the charm of Wimbledon. Queens is crowded and ghastly. There's no privacy at the club. The press can follow you anywhere. At Wimbledon the players have their own dining room. The press isn't allowed there, or in the changing rooms, or anywhere in the members' sectors of the All England Club. I know the reporters think this is too restrictive, and I sympathize to an extent, but it's awfully nice for the players to have some privacy.

I was unhappy the moment we got to Manhattan, and I stayed that way. We'd spent a week practicing on grass and relaxing by the sea at East Hampton on Long Island, the guests of an investment banker named Larry Baker. This was affluent, Great Gatsby territory, hardly typical American living, and the transition from the East Hampton preserve to Manhattan and Queens was a decided culture shock. We were afraid to walk very far from our hotel in Manhattan. Maybe we were overly cautious, but we'd read the scare stories about New York.

I was unhappy, and when I'm unhappy, I can't do much on a tennis court. I was seeded No. 2 behind Billie Jean. Chrissie, at No. 3, was in my half of the draw, and the build-up for the Evert-Goolagong rematch began.

It didn't last long. On the morning of his daughter Pam's third-round match, as Jerry Teeguarden was walking up Continental Avenue toward the West Side Club, he was approached by a man who handed him a calling card: Roland Koh, Bishop of West Malaysia. "God will be with you," the man said to Mr. Teeguarden and promptly drifted away.

Good vibrations? Who knows? Anyway, Jerry's tall, gangling daughter, Pam Teeguarden from Los Angeles, removed me, 7–5, 6–1. I was serving at 5–4, 40–15 in the first set, not playing well, but not having much trouble either. Pam canceled one set point by leaning into a forehand return. I hit a lousy forehand on the other. Deuce, and the fog was coming in fast on a bright, sunny day. That match slipped away faster than an Arab in Tel Aviv, as Pam won ten of the last eleven games from 3–5.

"Was that the 'walkabout' we've been hearing about?" the reporters asked.

"I don't know. I was just trying to run about . . . but I didn't get anywhere."

Billie Jean won the tournament over Kerry Melville, who upset Chrissie in the semis. Clearly Ms. King was No. 1 for 1972, and I was back again among the contenders.

We were going home, that was the main thing. It had been a long haul around the world, but the trip back was good: Disneyland, Hawaii, and the beaches of Fiji, my favorite place in the world.

There are more nerve-wracking things than playing tennis. Like calling on Queen Elizabeth at Buckingham Palace. Nothing in my upbringing prepared me for that. Queens have pretty much gone out of style, and Australians make light of royalty. But the fact is that when Queen Elizabeth visited Australia, everybody fell all over themselves to get a glimpse of her and make her welcome. Princess Anne's wedding was the biggest television event at home in years. Everybody seemed to become a royalist-for-a-day.

Queens don't have the power to chop off your head any more, but when I got an invitation to attend Her Majesty's garden party just after the 1972 Wimbledon, I felt like that day I had first explored Centre Court and gotten chopped up by Peaches Bartkowicz.

"It's all right, Evonne, I'll go with you," said Jenifer. You can't stay uptight with her around. Jen made the 1972 tour with me, then cut out with a gang of friends to live on a double-decker London bus painted purple. They roam Australia, stopping to work whenever they need money. I've joined them on my time off between tours, to have a marvelous time doing nothing but laughing and talking. Nobody mentions tennis. Jen would throw them out if they did, and she's capable, a sturdy girl.

"Just remember," Jen instructed. "Shouldn't say bloody this or bloody that to the queen. Those words aren't well received by English royalty."

"I wouldn't dream of . . ."

"I know," said Jen, "but a girl from the country is liable to be a little crude."

"Ah, Jen," I was laughing and forgetting my nerves.

"Do you think the queen knows you're fairly civilized? She probably thinks the Aborigines are still savage. But she'll be polite. She'll direct her flunkies to have platters of raw meat for you, and she'll have a couple of Scotland Yard men nearby to make sure you don't take a bite out of her . . ."

"Come off it, Jen."

A Rolls limousine showed up for us, and we were off to the palace, waving to everybody we passed.

It wasn't exactly intimate. Hundreds of people attend a queen's garden party. I don't know how she talks to all of them, but she gets around and says something to everybody. That's her job, and she's good at it.

When she got to us, I was so flustered I forgot everything I thought I might say. But she started it off. We curtsied and she did most of the talking. She said she'd seen me play on television, and she was very warm and gracious. I'd seen her on television too, but I didn't mention it. It wasn't a bad party, but it was too nerve-jangling for my taste.

Not long after that we were all invited back for the M.B.E. ceremonies. For my play in 1971, when I was also named the Female Athlete of the Year and Australian of the Year, I was placed on the Queen's Honors List for an M.B.E. I was proud and flattered. Other tennis players and athletes have been cited from time to time. Margaret Court, Virginia Wade, and Rod Laver have M.B.E.s. So does the Aboriginal boxer, Lionel Rose. I was pleased to get it. I knew it would mean a lot to my parents and the people of Barellan.

More nerves. I was about the youngest of scores of people in the Palace to be honored, and I kept worrying, "Will I do it right?"

Nothing to it, I might calm you future knights, commanders, and other decorateds-to-be. Somebody pushes you forward at the right time. The queen smiles, says something, and pins the decoration on, and somebody else pulls you away. It's an assembly line—with style and dignity. I worried about Jen and me not wearing hats, too. We never do. All the other women had on hats. All but the queen. Elizabeth, Evonne, and Jenifer were hatless. What a trio!

Later, at a reception, one of the officials, a chamberlain or something, said facetiously, "I hope you won't stand on any of the chairs, young lady."

But at the end, when I got separated from Jen and Mr. and Mrs. Edwards, there I was up on a chair whistling through my fingers to get their attention.

You can't take the country out of the girl, can you? Not even if she stops by the Palace to have tea with the queen.

When I got home, Mum said to me, "Well, I hope you haven't gone flash [conceited] just because you've been visiting with the queen. You don't mind having tea in the kitchen with us, do you?" Mum's idea of a celebrity is not Evonne Goolagong.

Her idea of a star is Kirk Douglas. At Forest Hills one afternoon I felt a tap on my shoulder, turned around, and there was Kirk "Spartacus" Douglas, real and unretouched. "Miss Goolagong," he said, "I just wanted to tell you how much I enjoy watching you play."

Quite nice and thoughtful, but before I could say, "Thank you, Mr. Douglas—you happen to be my Mum's favorite movie actor," he was gone. And I didn't even get his autograph for Mum, so I doubt she believes it happened.

From a story about Olga Morozova, the Russian, in *World Tennis* magazine: "Given the choice between Siberia and Akron, Ohio, Olga would undoubtedly choose Siberia. Unfortunately she's headed to Akron anyway, for the next tournament on the women's indoor circuit."

Akron was next. We were packing up to leave Hingham, Massachusetts, just outside of Boston, where I'd beaten Virginia Wade, 6–4,

6–4, to win my first U.S. title, the National Indoor. Virginia, a lithe, quick Englishwoman with dark hair and fine features, doesn't like to play me and I don't like to play her. We like each other fine, but on the court our inconsistencies bother each other. "She's infuriating to play against," Virginia says of me. "Always smiling whether she's winning or losing. You get the feeling she just doesn't give a damn, and it throws you off."

I never know how she'll play, she's so up and down, and that puts me off. When she's right, well, it doesn't matter how you play. She's got a thunderbolt serve and goes for everything. She can play out of her brain as she did in defeating me for the Australian title in 1972. We're mysteries to each other.

This was the beginning of 1973. I was in America for several indoor tournaments, and for the second time in my life I asked Mr. Edwards about tactics. The other time was against Evert at Wimbledon. Now it was for the unpredictable Wade. "Slice the ball to her backhand and come in behind that approach, sweet."

It worked like a dream, and I had one of the best volleying days of my life. Near the end of the first set, when I netted a volley, Virginia exclaimed to the audience, "Yippee—she actually missed one." But not many.

So it was off to Akron. Siberia might have been better. It was one of the coldest places I've ever been, in every way. I'm not anxious to go back, although the snow was fun. A blizzard struck the city, and I went out to romp in it with Janet Young, my doubles partner from Melbourne. We'd seen a bit of sleety snow before in England, but never the real thing that you could pack into snowballs and tramp through feeling like an Eskimo.

We felt we had to build a snowman. We did it all right, but the body was composed of big cubes of snow rather than the traditional spheres. Australian girls obviously can't be trusted to make a snowman properly.

Icier than the weather was the attitude of the woman in charge of the tournament, which was staged in a university gymnasium. I was beaten in the opening round by Marita Redondo, one of the horde of ball-blasting American teen-agers on the way up in tennis. You'd have thought I committed a crime. I was treated as though I'd thrown the match and had conspired to ruin their tournament, even though the crowds were excellent. Although I was out of the tournament and entitled to rest, I was commandeered to play in an exhibition mixed doubles one night and told that was the least I could do to atone for my defeat.

I'd never encountered treatment like it before, where I was blamed for allegedly hurting the tournament by losing. Everybody loses sometime. Nobody goes for years without defeat the way Suzanne Lenglen or Helen Wills did. There are more tough players and more tough tournaments today for one thing. Besides, upsets are a stimulating part of the game. Why shouldn't a promising kid like Redondo beat Goolagong? If tennis is too predictable it's dull.

But as tennis becomes more commercialized, a lot of the warmth may go out of it. Sponsors and promoters become overly concerned with their gates, and they may resent it when the leading players aren't in top form, even though they must realize it's impossible to maintain best form tournament after tournament. Margaret Court is the only one strong enough to come close to doing that. John Ballantine, in the *Sunday Times* of London, did some medical research to present a story asserting that Margaret is stronger than a majority of men. He may be right.

Even Margaret has letdowns. That's why I try to take frequent breaks to rest. I have to, and I suspect most players should. Or sometimes, if I'm not tired and want to play—not too hard—we'll find a small tournament where atmosphere is the primary concern and never mind the money. Like Kitzbühel in the Austrian Alps, a place and tournament I love. Or Lee-on-Solent in England.

There's so much money available on the pro circuits now that most women are reluctant to rest, even when they know they should. Californian Peggy Michel feels the women have gotten greedier than they were when she was first on the circuit five or six years ago. "They talk about two things, the weather—lousy—and the prize money—not enough," Peggy says. "The winners and the losers tend to gravitate to separate cliques. It's easy to get into a defeatist, what's-the-use mood when you hang with losers. The players are more selfish than they used to be, but I suspect all pro athletes are. They're looking out for themselves and know they have a limited time to make the big money.

"In the days when most of us were amateurs, we figured we'd play a couple of years, then quit. See the world, then go on to something else, probably marriage and family. Now that it's an occupation, women tend to stay at it longer, and the money becomes important. You're not just trying to make expenses on a few trips—you're earning your living.

"I was out for a while with hepatitis, and when I came back, nobody seemed particularly glad to see me. I was just one more player shooting for the money, somebody who might be hard to beat. Why should I be welcome?

"You can get awfully lonely playing pro tennis, and I don't think you have many real friends. You're lucky if you have a couple who have interests other than tennis, people you can talk to. It's all up to you in tennis. No help from anybody else like you get in a team game. If you don't win, you don't earn."

Peggy goes back further in the game than I do. She knows more of the players. She has a college degree, even though Billie Jean King told her, "You're a stupid fool for going to college. You're wasting time when you could be playing tournaments, and it'll be awful hard to catch up after you've graduated."

Peggy feels, "In terms of tennis development, Billie Jean was probably right, but I'm glad I have my degree. The circuit can be very narrow. In a sense we're pioneers. Pro tennis as a recognized career for women only goes back to 1968. We still don't have complete public recognition as devoted career women. Billie Jean has been one of the most influential in changing attitudes. She says, 'Look at us as pro athletes, just as you would a baseball or football player. Some are pretty, some are not, but we should be judged on performance not looks. Do people ask if a tackle on a football team is handsome? No, they just want to know if he can block, do his job. There's still a double standard. Reporters ask me about my abortion, but would they inquire about a male athlete's vasectomy?'

"Billie Jean's a right-on gal, a militant feminist. Few come on as strong as she does, but without her we wouldn't have advanced so far."

Because I've practically always traveled with the Edwardses, I haven't spent too much time with the other players. I haven't gotten the feeling of a cutthroat business the way some of them have, and I hope I never do. But I do feel uncomfortable among losers: I've tried to stay aloof from the power struggles and still be friendly with everyone. I'm happy that beginning in 1974 there was one women's prize money circuit in the U.S., with the Virginia Slims organization cooperating with the USLTA in the promotion. The split seemed healed.

Whether the promoters and players will become a hardened lot as the money grows in volume and importance I don't know. Akron, I should say, was a decided exception to the wonderful way I've been treated throughout the world. I just hope it wasn't a hint of things to come when winning is absolutely everything.

When in Rome, do as the Romans do: scream your sunburnt head off for any Italian tennis player. Peel your shirt. Let your inhibitions hang out. Swill wine. Gobble marvelous ice cream. Ogle signorinas in chic T-shirts or signores in trim ensembles. I doubt that any tournament is more fun than the Italian Open, a seven-rectangle circus far removed spiritually from the cathedral of Wimbledon. The jubilant screamers at Il Foro Italico could be crowds at a soccer, hockey, or baseball game. The English may have invented tennis, but the Italians have humanized it.

When an Italian is playing an alien, the crowd pulls their countryman along with their vocal chords. Their bravos shake even the huge jockstrapped statues of ancient Roman athletes that stand guard over Campo Centro, the main court of this handsome tennis complex beside the Tiber.

I suppose it's nice to have Wimbledon as a contrast in mode and mood. Wimbledon: hushed, reverent, organized like any British pageant, functioning as faultlessly as a Swiss watch. The Italian: loud, boisterous, casual, and often frantic, functioning as smoothly as . . . uh . . . an Italian tennis tournament.

How had I stayed away so long? My first taste of Il Foro was in 1973, and I found it the nicest, most pleasant place for tennis. I was happy and relaxed. When I'm happy I play well. What a change from Forest Hills, not to mention Akron. Barry Newcombe, of the London *Evening Standard,* may call Campo Centro the "punishment pit" because of the grueling matches on slow clay, frequently in extreme heat, sometimes with a partisan gallery acclaiming an alien's every mistake against an Italian. But look around. See how fine the place is. It puts you in a romantic state of mind, loose and dreamy. All those billow-topped pines forming an emerald tiara for Il Foro; a hill of greenery, Monte Mario, overseeing the marble amphitheater; grassy slopes descending to the six outside courts; outdoor cafes; sequestered plots of lawn where you can steal a nap; the Tiber gurgling nearby; overpowering statuary; total warmth; all distinctively Roman despite the absence of fountains.

Since Il Foro was built during the dictatorship of Benito Mussolini, you would have to credit him with more than just making the trains run on time. Mussolini, who prided himself on his fitness, played tennis, and a story is told of his fondness for hitting forehands and the hell with everything else. In Italian, forehand is *diritto,* which also means forward. In that day, one of the favored Fascist slogans was *"noi tireremo diritto"* (we must go forward). One day at the dictator's court at Villa Torlonia, his instructor, Mario Belardinelli, hit the usual quota to the boss's forehand to make him look good, then suggested some work on Il Duce's *rovescio,* the backhand.

"Belardinelli," growled Mussolini, projecting his chin in his best balcony manner, "remember—*noi tireremo diritto!"*

During his regime the place was named Il Foro Mussolini, and he was very proud of this elegant playground. He should have been. Where it's a physical struggle to observe a match on courts outside of the stadium at Wimbledon, Forest Hills, or Roland Garros, Il Foro offers a pleasant hillside for those who wish to sit in at the six courts away from Campo Centro, plus a balcony with a restaurant above Courts One and Two. You can watch four matches at once while devouring a salad in the players' dining room.

I don't know whether it's characteristic of the Italian temperament or just an amusing tale I was told about an old man named Alberto Foleno that illustrates their capriciousness. Foleno, well past his playing days, comes to Il Foro as an eager spectator now. Though not a famous player, he deserves a mention in Italian tennis history, a man who disdained a victory that seemed too easy. Years ago, on the verge of scoring a big win at Viareggio, Foleno was confronted, at match point, by a sitter at the net. The match was his, yet instead of putting the ball away he caught it, thus losing the point. Too simple and drab—he didn't want to win it that way. Presently he lost. His was a carefree gesture that would be inconceivable to a pro today.

If Rome was joyous for me, I doubt that her first visit was very gratifying to Chrissie Evert, who couldn't quite nail down a major championship. In 1973 she was in the finals of three of the biggest— Wimbledon, France, and Italy—and lost them all, to King, Court, and me. Since the 1972 Wimbledon she'd murdered me: five straight, and naturally she was favored in the Italian final on slow clay where she's more at home than a crab in sand. Her last four wins over me had been on clay, three in her native Florida on the U.S. spring circuit, shortly before Rome.

But Rome and I were in love. Mrs. Edwards and I walked the narrow streets, explored piazzas and ruins. I took home a few pieces of stone from a ruin later and gave them to Mum. She immediately put them away in a special drawer.

I was happy and hitting the ball as well as I could. We planned to go to the Catacombs one day, but I was scheduled late in the afternoon for my semifinal against the Czechoslovak, Vlasta Vopickova, sister of Jan Kodes. "You've got to pay attention to business and win fast or the Catacombs will be closed and we'll miss it this trip," warned Mrs. Edwards. It took me twenty-nine minutes to beat Vlasta,

6–2, 6–1. "You see, if you put your mind to something and keep it there . . . ," Mrs. Edwards said as we trotted to a taxi.

One thing about Rome is a little scary: when you leave the women's changing room to go to Campo Centro, you walk down a long dark tunnel until—all at once—you're in a vast arena, an enclosure much larger than Centre Court, with people buzzing on all sides. For a moment you think you're one of the Christians sent in with the beasts.

Rome was my town, and I was delighted to be her champion. I was also honored to notice that the leading Italian reporters, Rino Tommasi, Gianni Clerici, and Alfonso (Foom) Fumarola, were in the press stand and even awake. Italians' regard for women's tennis is about as high as their demand for New York State wine. "Ah, but we have to watch such lovely ladies who hit the ball so well," said Clerici, of Milan.

Rome was not such a joyful place for Ilie Nastase, even though he became the first to hold the U.S., French, and Italian titles at one time. "These people are not so nice," said the Bucharest Buffoon several times. Perhaps his viewpoint was warped by the curses—and a bottle—hurled at him, as well as by the intruder who ventured into the dressing room in the hope of slugging him.

Maybe Nastase brings a lot of it on himself with his antics. He would be better off, too, if he didn't speak and understand Italian. Rome began to be too much for Ilie when he opposed Ezio di Matteo in the second round. The local boy had the crowd backing him, as expected. Not only were they with di Matteo, but they were on Nastase. Fiercely.

One strident customer kept shouting, *"Uccidelo!"* (kill him). Ilie, understanding, stopped playing and asked the fellow why he was so vicious.

"Because I bet 10,000 lire [$17] on di Matteo," was the straightforward reply. It was a bad bet (Ilie won, 6–0, 6–3), but the price was right, 6 to 1 fresh off the morning line of the tournament program editor Rino (The Roman) Tommasi, the Eternal City's answer to Jimmy (The Greek) Snyder of Las Vegas. Surely Tommasi's is the only tennis program containing a daily betting line on every match, and probably the only sports program of any kind to offer such a service aside from the established gambling pastimes (horses, dogs, and jai alai). "It is illegal, true," concedes Tommasi, who also publishes the Italian tennis magazine, *Tennis Club.* "But people will gamble anyway here, so we may as well furnish the odds."

After his trouble with the di Matteo fans, the day deteriorated fast for Nastase. He and Jimmy Connors walked out on a doubles against Patrice Dominguez and Wanaro N'Godrella, of France, even though they were leading, 6–4, 2–1. "These people call us everything —bastards . . . clowns . . . and we aren't even playing against Italians," griped Nastase. From then on it was Rome versus Romanian.

In Nastase's semifinal against the last of the locals, the Pasta Kid (Paolo Bertolucci, a little round man with an excellent touch), Campo Centro was in pandemonium as Bertolucci caught up in the fourth set. Nastase was being cheated by patriotic linesmen, and the crowd was whooping it up, chanting "PAO-LO! PAO-LO!" over and over. Did they incite Ilie, or vice versa? He was justifiably angered when they gave him bad calls on the lines. Who knows what the spectators and Nastase were saying to each other? Whatever it was, it wasn't pleasant.

Abruptly he spat toward the seats. Down came a bottle with a violent flood of jeers and the demand, *"Fuori . . . fuori!"* (throw him out). Would the police be necessary? They stood in the wings, no strangers to a tennis court in Rome. Nastase walked to the bottle, picked it up and put it in his pocket. He was a little disappointed. No style to the thrower. Not only was the bottle empty, but it was a mineral water bottle.

You'd think they'd throw a champagne bottle at an artist like Nastase—a full bottle.

Even though they didn't like him—for the moment—Romans had to accept the fact that they had a new emperor, a genius on strings who could fiddle while they burned.

Ilie and I departed with varying affection for Rome, but we both came away with the championships of Italy.

If 1972 was a disappointment to many of my followers, I don't think they could feel let down over 1973. It was my steadiest year. Even though I didn't win one of the Big Four, I was finalist to Margaret Court at the Australian and U.S.; semifinalist to the champ, Billie Jean King, at Wimbledon; and semifinalist to the champ, Court, at the French. Besides the Italian, U.S. Indoor, and the Canadian singles titles, I won ten other tournaments out of a total of twenty-nine. I was runner-up twelve times, semifinalist three times, and otherwise lost only that first rounder at Akron.

Court was still my heroine and my hex. A point here or there and I might have won the Australian and U.S. from her. In the New South Wales final at Sydney I served twice for the match, a steaming battle at White City in which she outlasted me, 4–6, 6–3, 10–8.

That one was too much for Barry Court and Mr. Edwards. They retreated from their seats to pace outside the stadium, peeking through an opening periodically at the scoreboard. Margaret says she doesn't care a thing for Women's Lib, but Billie Jean insists, "Court is Women's Lib in action. She goes out and earns the bread [over $200,000 in 1973 prize money] while Barry takes care of the kid."

Whatever, there was Barry carrying their son, Danny, who was asleep, during his vigil outside the stadium with Mr. Edwards. They must have been quite a sight. "What's the score, Barry?" Mr. Edwards would be puffing away. "I can't look."

"You hold Danny a while, please, Vic. I need a cigarette." So Mr. Edwards would take over the baby-lugging.

Forest Hills was better than the previous year. Instead of staying in a Manhattan hotel, we rented a house in Forest Hills Gardens, an attractively landscaped enclave within walking distance of the West Side Tennis Club. Although Queens may not have the well-preserved suburban peace and beauty of Wimbledon, Forest Hills Gardens came close. We didn't go into the city much, and I guess I practiced more because I got bored sitting around.

There were no problems until the semis when I did the old fade after winning the first set from the German, Helga Masthoff, and

183

didn't come out of it until 1–4 in the third, winning the last five games. The crowd groaned at my every mistake and began booting me home with shouts of "Come on, Goolie!" near the end. Poor Helga, a six-footer as lovely as a swan, I'd done practically the same thing to her at Toronto in the final of the Canadian Open. There she led 5–1 in the first before losing, 7–6, 6–4.

Against Margaret in the Forest Hills final, I was off to 4–1, flying, serving splendidly and doing it all. She was slow in starting and was down 0–40 in the sixth game. Three break points, and I let them go, blowing a simple backhand volley on the third. She drew even and went ahead 6–5, but I broke her to get into the tie-breaker. Which I squandered immediately, missing an easy smash and double faulting. She had a 2–0 lead and won it 5–2. I won the second set, but in her fashion, Marg just got tougher and cruised away with the third and the championship—and $25,000. Barry smiled, "Marg never said that the women should get the same money as the men" (whose first prize, won by John Newcombe, was also $25,000). "But I believe she'll cash the check."

What could Goolagong and Evert do for an encore at Wimbledon 1973? Well, we might have staged a rematch of that nerve-jangling 1972 semi—only this time as a final. I had the feeling we would do just that. Chrissie made it, but I didn't. Billie Jean cut me off at the semis, 6–3, 5–7, 6–3, and then annihilated Chrissie, 6–0, 7–5. Ms. King was on her Wimbledon warpath again.

I wasn't far out of high gear myself all the way to the semis, losing no sets, bombing through Virginia Wade in the quarters, 6–3, 6–3.

I got up the morning of the semi and said hesitantly, "I don't know . . ." to Mr. Edwards. Every day I'd had that good feeling. Until this day. I fought Billie Jean off all the way, playing my best when I was cornered. She served for the match at 5–4 in the second and had two match points that I killed with backhands. That stalled her and I won three games for the set. I got to 3–2 on serve in the third, but she tore away to win the last four games.

We'll both remember the very last game for a long time. I was serving and it was a feast of all-out shots and saves on both sides of the net as we went to deuce six times. She stacked up the match points and I knocked them over, five of them. On the sixth I served and roared in, poking my backhand volley barely beyond the baseline. Billie Jean was safely through and continued to her fifth Wimbledon title.

I had invaded Chris Evert's territory, America, four times and now, in December of 1973, it was her turn to make her longest journey, to my island, for the Bell Cup just after Christmas and then the 1974 Australian Open. Both would be on grass, the Bell Cup at White City in Sydney and the Open at Kooyong in Melbourne. Australians had read much about "The Little Machine"—Olga Morozova's nickname for Chris—and were anxious to see her for the first time, hopefully against me and Margaret Court.

The Bell Cup was put into competition in 1972 by an enthusiastic hacker from Cleveland, Jess Bell, head of Bonne Bell Cosmetics, intended as the prize for an annual match between American and Australian women. Although Chris beat both me and Margaret, those were the only two points for the U.S. as we won the inaugural in Cleveland, 5–2.

For 1973 the format was changed to best-of-nine matches, Mr. Edwards was named our captain, and we were jolted by the withdrawal of Margaret, who announced her second pregnancy. We were further jolted when Julie Heldman beat me, 6–3, 1–6, 6–3, in my opening singles on the second day, and Janet Newberry overcame Kerry Harris, 4–6, 7–6, 6–4, to put the Americans ahead, 3–2. Lesley Hunt and I salvaged something with a 6–3, 6–1 doubles win over Chris Evert and Nancy Gunter, so we were deadlocked 3–3 going into the last day.

Maybe I was looking forward to Chris too much after I'd won the second set from Heldman and led 3–1 in the third. No time for walkabout against an opponent as crafty and competitive as Julie.

Whatever, I was a little peeved with myself. I was playing for Australia for the first time in Sydney, with my friends and some of my family watching. It wasn't just another tournament. This was a match that could give Australia an extraordinary clean sweep of the major trophies. Back in the spring, at Bad Hamburg, West Germany, Patty Coleman, Janet Young, and I had won the Federation Cup for Australia. I maintained my unbeaten singles record (9-0) for three years of Federation Cup as we defeated Japan, Indonesia, West Germany, and, finally, the defending champion, South Africa in the worldwide team tournament. Also that spring Ken Rosewall spurred Australia to a 5-2 win over the U.S. in the World Cup at Hartford, an annual team match for male pros between our countries. Then, as December began, Rod Laver and John Newcombe regained the Davis Cup for Australia in a 5-0 crushing of the U.S. at Cleveland.

It remained for us women to complete the four-way sweep by keeping the Bell Cup.

It was precisely that—a sweep—on the final day. I was at the peak of my game in beating Chris, 6-2, 6-3, and we concluded the 6-3 victory with Kerry Melville battling back to stop Heldman, 2-6, 6-1, 6-4, and Janet Young and I beating Pam Teeguarden and Janet Newberry, 6-2, 6-3.

Not since our competitive introduction at Wimbledon the year before had Chris and I met on grass. I was 2-0 against her on my favorite footing as we flew to Melbourne, and I was confident that if I played my way—attacking her constantly—I could beat her for' the Australian championship. There was no doubt in my mind that Chris would be in the final, and sure enough, there she was, without losing a set.

When we arrived at Kooyong, Mr. Edwards and I—and everybody else—were keenly aware of his prediction of years before: "1974 will be Evonne's year. She'll have matured physically and mentally to the point where she could and should win all the major titles and be No. 1. Anything else she accomplishes prior to that will be gravy."

There had been plenty of gravy, but 1974 was a few days away, and despite my successes on other continents I'd never won the championship of my own country. I'd won France, Italy, Britain (Wimbledon), and the U.S. Indoor as well as the singles titles of eight other countries. I'd also won the Australian Hard Court (clay), but not the Australian title on grass, a jewel in the Big Four, first leg of the Grand Slam. Margaret had frustrated me in the finals of 1971 and 1973, and Virginia Wade in the final of 1972.

This time Margaret was absent, expecting another child. But Chris was here, and she still held a 6–4 edge in our rivalry. It had been a fine, yet agonizing year for her in losing three successive major finals —France, Italy, and Wimbledon. At last she won one, South Africa, paying me back for Italy.

While Chris was breezing to the final, knocking over her Bell Cup teammates Newberry and Heldman in the quarters and semis, I was being jostled by my countrywomen. Karen Krantzcke was stubborn in the quarters, 4–6, 6–3, 6–2; then Kerry Melville, 7–6, 5–7, 6–1.

The first day of the new year was bright and hot and joyous. There must have been oceans of grog consumed in New Year's Eve celebrations across the city, but people were ready to celebrate some more at Kooyong where an overflow crowd of 13,000 settled into the concrete bowl to bake and barrack for two Aussies—Phil Dent and me—against two Yanks—Chris and her fiancé, Jimmy Connors—in the finals. Melbourne can be formal, even for tennis. In the expensive seats, men wore jackets and ties, and women draped themselves in flowery dresses and broad hats, as though to show the world that Wimbledon custom could be maintained by the good folk of this ex-colony at the bottom of the world. But in the east stands, general admissions, kids let their bellies and legs and bare feet hang out, and had a gay old time drinking beer from their eskies (portable coolers).

As long as the beer—and Phil Dent and I—held out, they'd stay happy. It was Phil Dent and his doubles partner, John Alexander, who made, in chorus, a statement that typifies Australians. Parched at the end of a long match a couple of years ago, they gasped, "We're so thirsty we'd drink water."

Denty didn't make it that day, losing to Connors in four sets. But I did, closing with the charge of my life to win, 7–6, 4–6, 6–0.

Chris and I stayed together serve for serve to 4–4, where she broke me and served for the first set. I broke back, and took the tie-breaker, and the set, 7–5.

"Get to the net," I kept telling myself, but in the second set I didn't budge from the baseline. I thought I could beat Chris in her style, too, as I'd done at Cincinnati. Not quite. I couldn't quite match her groundies, although the rallies were stimulating and exciting. One set each, and we went to the changing room for a shower and dry clothing.

As I came out, ready to resume play, Mr. Edwards stopped me. "Evonne . . ." I'd never heard him so emotional. He was trembling. "Evonne, play your game . . . your game. You must attack." He'd watched me lose this final three times. I wondered if he could stand it again—at the beginning of his year of prophecy.

"Honey . . ." We were walking to the entrance to the broad, green enclosure which he could not enter. He would have to return to his seat. "Evonne, honey . . . please . . . believe in God . . . believe in yourself . . . believe in me . . ."

Then we were on. I was tingling. I guess you'd call it a fire-and-brimstone pep talk. He'd never spoken to me that way. I didn't run through a wall to get at Chris, or anything like that. I don't think I looked any different. But I knew I had to win this for him, to attack, attack, attack, and keep my mind on it from the first point.

There weren't many points. Just six games. Chris got only nine points as I drove my approaches to the corners and flew in for the volleys. I served and volleyed, lived at the net. In little over a quarter of an hour I heard the umpire call, "Game, set, and championship to Miss Goolagong . . ." And I felt something drift onto my head. Confetti, streamers, saved up from the parties of the previous evening, floated down to the court. Everybody was up and cheering. It went on . . . and on. I'm sure "Chocolata" Goolagong was blushing red.

When would they stop clapping? Not for five minutes, according to the journalists who timed it. It was a regular waratah (party) in the stadium. On a value scale I suppose Wimbledon, the U.S., and the French titles rate higher than the Australian. But when you've dreamed about being champion of your country for thirteen years, nothing could feel quite so good.

But I won't take all this too seriously. How can I with a wonderful Mum like mine? "You know, Evonne," she said when I was visiting Barellan recently, "they've named a little park for you down by the railroad. Goolagong Park, ain't that nice?" A couple of picnic tables and some grass and a toilet.

"You've really done something for Barellan, Evonne. Because of you we've got our first public dunny!"

The original Australians have a champion of Australia: I hope the first of many.

I am several identities—woman, Aborigine, professional athlete, Australian—and I delight in them all. But first I am Australian. An Aborigine knows better than most that nothing is permanent. I'll just keep moving until I can't any more. Looking for sustenance, which for me is tennis. Though I am as much a product of white Australian civilization as I am of my bloodline, I know I will never still the ancestral cry: "Keep moving."

I will travel the world tournament circuit and see America with the Pittsburgh Triangles. Winning, losing, charging, and walkabouting . . . but always moving.

From the trickle of the Sandy, Mirool, and Colinroobie . . . to the rush of the Allegheny, Monongahela, and Ohio . . .

From the hush of Barellan where they use sheep for lawn mowers . . . to the roar of Pittsburgh and the other industrial cities of the world where tennis has taken hold . . .

From the day I turned twenty on a court at Hilversum in the Netherlands and 4,000 spectators surprised me by singing "Happy Birthday" (and I wondered what they were doing because it was Dutch to me) . . . to the tickertape parade through Sydney after I returned from winning Wimbledon, and the car I was riding caught fire . . .

From a tin shack on Bendee Street where I drank too much gasoline one day and almost ended the story before it began . . . to Buckingham Palace and a drink of tea with Elizabeth Windsor . . .

From running barefoot across wheatfields, chasing rabbits . . . to chasing a tennis ball up and down and around the globe for as long as my legs and my brain shout, "Geronimo!"

I hope that's a long time. It will end someday, I know. I don't think I'll cry when it's ended, but I might.

In the meantime, I'll keep moving . . . always moving.